Family
Networks

ROSS V. SPECK
CAROLYN L. ATTNEAVE

PANTHEON BOOKS   A Division of Random House, New York

Library of Congress Cataloging in Publication Data

Speck, Ross V.
Family Networks.
            (World of Man)
  1. Family social work. 2. Family psychotherapy.
3. Social group work. I. Attneave, Carolyn L.,
joint author. II. Title. [DNLM: 1. Psychotherapy,
Group. WM 430 S741r 1973]
HV43.S64   616.8'915   72–12836
ISBN 0–394–48090–2

Manufactured in the United States of America by the Haddon Craftsmen, Inc., Scranton, Pa.

9 8 7 6 5 4 3 2

First Edition

Contents

Acknowledgments

DURING 1970 Salvador Minuchin, director of the Philadelphia Child Guidance Clinic, provided an opportunity for us to work collaboratively for five months while introducing his staff to social network intervention techniques. It was then that this book was first conceived, and hence we name him as one of its godfathers.

Jay Haley is another, and his interest in early drafts of the work and his sharp powers of condensation resulted in the publication of a chapter in his own *Changing Families,* which has been reproduced in Ferber *et al.*'s *The Book of Family Therapy* and in Sager and Kaplan's *Progress in Group and Family Therapy,* Vol. I.[1]

Godmother to this volume is Sara Blackburn, whose sensitive editing and tactful skills at excising redundancies made the completion of the book a pleasure.

Jerome Olans and Uri Rueveni deserve our thanks as

[1]Jay Haley, ed., *Changing Families: A Family Therapy Reader* (New York: Grune & Stratton, 1971); reprinted by permission. Andrew Ferber, Marilyn Mendelsohn, and Augustus Napier, eds., *The Book of Family Therapy* (New York: Science House, 1972). Clifford Sager and Helen Singer Kaplan, eds., *Progress in Group and Family Therapy* (New York: Brunner/Mazel, 1972), vol. 1.

members of our intervention teams in numerous social network meetings.

Katherine Orner typed the bulk of the original manuscript and we appreciate her sticking to the task under far from ideal conditions.

It is fitting that we thank those social networks that we have assembled. Even though we cannot take space to name them, we hope they will continue to keep us posted on their further adventures.

We owe much, too, to our own families, clans, tribes, and social networks. In essence what we have to say in this book was learned first from them, and we hope they are not too surprised to discover how we have used what they taught us.

Finally we owe a special acknowledgment to the network of our colleagues, whose interest, challenge, and support cannot be valued in words alone. We hope they will find themselves on this network chart, and recognize its nonverbal messages.

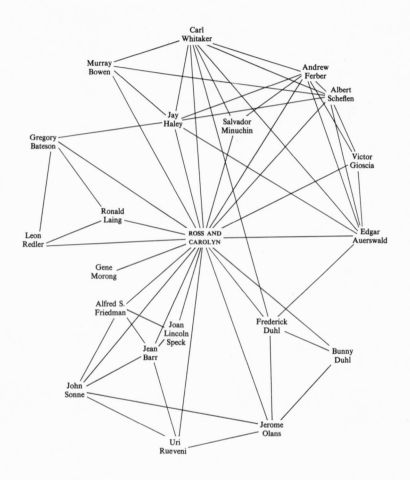

THE NETWORK OF THOSE WHO ACTIVELY
SUPPORTED, INSPIRED, AND SOMETIMES
RESTRAINED US IN THE PREPARATION OF THIS
BOOK

Introduction

I AM ROSS, sometimes a *metaperson* on purpose. Not that one has much chance or choice in being something other than what he is. I was born into a large family (and family network) in a small town in southern Ontario, Canada. My parents and their parents came from small farms. My father quit school in the fourth grade to hire himself out with his two horses to help build a canal. A few years later the tractor was invented and the horses were no longer useful for making a living; so he moved to the nearby small city where he spent his life pumping gasoline behind a car, rather than walking behind a horse.

Memories of Sundays and some weeknights in the revivalist fundamentalist church, tent revivals, and salvation meetings kindled a strong interest in the energies that accumulate between large groups of people. Annual family reunions—when four generations of the clan arrived for a day of picnicking, games, gossip, and petty family squabbles among the 200 or so persons who sometimes attended—provided an additional glimpse of some potentials for healing, helping, hearing, and even disturbing the routine boredom of everyday family interaction.

As a young boy 30 or 40 years ago, I developed the habit of withdrawing into myself in fantasy whenever the pain of everyday existence, boredom, or frustration seemed too great. These trips into myself were rarely painful or unpleasant and were not accompanied by a great deal of anxiety or fear. A year that I spent in bed when I was about ten had a useful result in terms of developing an identity about what I was *not* going to do with my life. In some of my deliberate states of withdrawal, I experienced forces or energies that at times made me tremble. They were accompanied by "great" insights that left me with a sense of well-being—a sense of being renewed and tranquil. From what I now know, I was experimenting with the fringes of *prophetic beingness,* which I feel sure is in every person if he cares to open the door.

Without many books or much family encouagement, I was a dedicated student and found myself being assigned to medical school by the local high school principal, who was perturbed because I had made no definite college plans. His plan was acceptable because I had no other alternatives, and I'd always felt a mission to help people.

Internship, during which many of my patients seemed to die, subverted my goal of becoming a country doctor. I went into psychiatry out of curiosity about myself and others, but also with a conviction that there were an awful lot of people who needed help. Two periods of army service (a choice forced by Canada and later by the USA) convinced me that all societal institutions, from the family to the army, were dedicated in an authoritarian way to the nonrealization of most human potentials.

Four years of psychiatric residency taught me to interview and diagnose the patient who was regarded as sick and requiring treatment. I learned to give electric and insulin shocks, put people in strait jackets, wet packs, continuous baths (hydrotherapy), and needle-point showers. Dunking had gone out by then. Sedatives, stimulants, belladonna alkaloids, and, later, phenothiazines and other tranquilizers were popular methods to "treat" the mental hospital patient. For a time I was assigned to care for postlobotomy patients on the surgical ward. I can remember a number of these poor souls when infection or increased intracranial pressure intervened and forced the cerebral cortex and underlying brain tissue through the bilateral burrholes, so that it appeared that the person had three-or four-inch horns growing out of his head. (Shades of demonology!) Along with all of the biological somatic treatments came exposure to psychotherapy, with supervision and group psychotherapy.

The psychotherapies seemed useful to certain patients at least and also seemed to obey the old adage of physicians, *primum non nocere* (first of all, do no harm). So I decided to become a psychotherapist. In order to get the best existing training, I started my personal psychoanalysis and enrolled in a psychoanalytic institute, from which I was graduated seven and one-half years later. Meanwhile, I was a research psychiatrist and psychotherapist who met with several hundred families, each of whom contained a diagnosed schizophrenic between the ages of 15 and 30. These people were all treated by family therapy in their own homes. The goal was to modify the socially shared psychopathology, to prevent hospitalization if at all possible, and to remove the stigma of the schizophrenic label from one person in the family.

In about four cases out of five, some of these goals were reached more rapidly than in our previous experience working in one-to-one therapy with the symptomatic person. The mode of treatment was psychotherapy; no medication was used. In about 20 percent of the cases, however, scapegoating, double-binds, mystification, sick-role reinforcement, etc., seemed to arise from outside the nuclear family unit. When we included extended family members in family treatment, we encountered frequent resistance. It was becoming apparent that the symptomatic condition called schizophrenia was part of a constellation of disturbed role relationships such as symbiosis—mutual binds of love and hate—and other abnormalities in all members of the family and frequently in their friends, neighbors, and relatives as well. By 1964, I had begun to investigate, study, and experiment with various combinations of *significant others* as a part of the ongoing family therapy for treating schizophrenia. A short time later I read Elizabeth Bott's *Family and Social Network*. This supplied ideas for the more systematic study of the social network of the schizophrenic family.

By 1966, I had assembled the first schizophrenic family network, and an average of 40 persons attended weekly meetings for about the next nine months. My goals were to facilitate resocialization of the family unit—which had become quite isolated from its friends, relatives, and neighbors—by demystifying family and network secrets and collusions, and by trying to disrupt pathological binds between persons, and at the same time to strengthen healing bonds.

Enough success was achieved with this network to begin another network intervention. The long period of time I spent with the first network had the advantage of letting me see practically every emergency, continuum, and unexpected event that could occur within it. I began to realize that I had operated with one foot on the accelerator and the other foot just as strongly on the brake. In succeeding networks, the amount of time for the intervention has been reduced to six weeks, and in some cases to three meetings at fortnightly intervals. A couple of networks were attempted in a single long evening session. I also began experimenting with the use of network intervention in professional organizations and using network simulation as a teaching method.

At the present time, I am investigating with the London

Association the psychology of fun and madness. We are planning to establish a Fun House (reverse madhouse), where "normal" families and networks can come to expand their awareness of themselves and of the community. A by-product of this endeavor may be the establishment of a self-help therapeutic community, as well as further explorations into altered states of consciousness, including an investigation of the energies involved in prophecy.

I AM CAROLYN. I was born in El Paso, Texas, to an unlikely confluence of family strains. My mother's people were Delaware Indians who wandered purposefully away from tribal roots in order to make money to support tribal affairs. Mother attended boarding school, but one for well-to-do white girls, not a Bureau of Indian Affairs school. Dad's folks were similarly detached from their roots. His mother emigrated from Sweden in her teens, and his father was one of those Texans whose antecedants were neither revealed nor questioned. My aunts and uncles on both sides knew one another from high school days, and family ties seemed close, but stretched by distance, as our family went west to California in my infancy. Much closer ties persisted between my parents and a number of friends who became "uncles" or acted like "aunts" as we traveled around.

The family inheritance of restlessness seemed perpetual. Two years was my longest residence in any one community until I was past 30. This experience of rambling about the West, with its heritage of Spanish-speaking and Oriental populations, was interwoven with several childhood visits of six, nine, and twelve months with my mother's family in the Southwest. I had lots of opportunity to observe many subcultures and to be aware not only of how similar people were, but also how many ways there were to arrange relationships.

Friendships, families, school organizations, town affairs—all had to be studied for their own patterns. When I had identified similarities and differences, I could join in. I learned, for instance, that every school put on plays and that acting roles went to hometown people who were known, but that managing and technical help were welcomed. Often it was easy to size things up quickly because we were in small towns and little cities. I could quickly identify and exchange recognition signals with nearly everyone. Stratifications, roles, patterns of association, and customs were obvious but not binding on newcomers, who often brought together people who would otherwise not "see" one another as whole people. Communal efforts in times of flood or tornado, neighborliness in times of illness and death, as well as the shared celebration of births, weddings, and holidays were all real and visible phenomena. The people in every community did the same things in different ways.

I also had the opportunity to observe the social patterns of academia because, while I was earning my way, I moved through five different colleges. I was aware during those years of what I did not want to do. I resisted everyone's efforts to push me into being a schoolteacher, even though this seemed to be one of the few options for a girl to follow if she went to college. I was vaguely aware that my parents felt law or medicine were too sordid for a "lady," and I never explored these possibilities because I couldn't see how I could afford the training they required. Perhaps the same blinders kept me from recognizing that a profession called social work existed.

I encountered psychology and sociology after several years' immersion in literature and the arts. These fields presented a view of childhood, family, and social relationships that made sense out of my own observations and suggested that there were other ways of growing up than I had experienced. The threads of social and individual development seemed to me most interestingly intertwined in the lives of children and families during the elementary and preschool years, although this was not a recognized field at this time. I moved from school counseling to clinical, child, and finally family therapy in what seemed a natural and practical progression, while I was doing graduate work and later supporting my own family.

Although most of my skipping about from place to place was in the far West and Southwest, two-year sojourns in Florida, Washington, D.C., and Mississippi added experience with black communities and stratified southern families. I also became involved with blind and retarded children and with the rehabilitation of blind, deaf, and paraplegic adults, which deepened my appreciation of the interdependent needs and strengths in the social matrix surrounding and supporting all of us as we face problems and enjoy living.

As I worked with children, families, teachers, and students, I felt a strong need to assess strengths on which to build, rather than merely ferreting out pathology—so that for me a clinical "diagnosis" became a two-part affair. The first task was developing a profile of characteristics within the individual, showing both strengths as well as weaknesses; then I felt the necessity of matching these strengths and weaknesses to the resources available in the community. The goal for me was to build coherent relationships between persons who could stimulate each other and provide maximum reciprocal growth. This led to the development of treatment teams made up of local people significant in the lives of my so-called patients. Where needed and available, other professionals were incorporated. Social workers, speech pathologists, teachers, psychiatrists, physicians, probation officers, and public health nurses were often involved. The team did not stop here but often stretched out to include clergymen, scout leaders, neighbors, storekeepers, relatives, and anyone else who was in contact with the family and had a contribution to make.

What else could one do, for example, with a nine-year-old schizophrenic girl for whom there would be no room in a treatment facility for two or three years? And so her small town became what I suppose others would call the "treatment milieu." When she was *in contact,* she learned and developed emotionally, and when she was out on her own personal cloud nine, she was protected. High school youngsters would steer her back to school, storekeepers would calmly arrange for her to handle their goods and would buffer her from intrusive customers until someone could come to take her home. Teachers found that they could show how pleased they were with what she could learn. They also became flexible about assignments, grades, and achievement. In ways like these, her parents were relieved of a private burden and were supported in their own context. This wasn't a perfect solution—but it seemed to me then as close an approximation of the ideal residential treatment described in the literature as was available. And, from a practical standpoint, it was far less expensive.

There were some parallel personal developments to these professional strides along new paths. During the 1950's, I realized that while I might be a nomad forever as an individual, I needed roots if I was to successfully raise a couple of children. We were a one-parent family with a four- and a five-year-old. There were no real kinfolk for thousands of miles when we set about creating a family of our own. We began with St. Christopher's Parish in Lubbock, Texas, and developed what I would now call a social network complete with an adopted grandmother, aunts and uncles for me, aunts and uncles for the kids (who became sisters and brothers for me), cousins, friends, colleagues, teachers, neighbors, and even people we didn't get along with. That six-year period of deep and meaningful relationships has established Lubbock as "home" for all three of us, and the same feelings persist today, parallel to, and as authentic as, the warmth between us and our few remaining real, but scattered, relatives.

When we moved again for a six-year period to Oklahoma, we gained experience in holding on to relationships over distance, but we also felt the need to repair holes in the network fabric. We adopted another grandmother and another brother for me, who could be avuncular to the kids, and we gained some additional experience with Indian families who added their own versions of informal adoptive ties. These were our first contacts with Indian families outside my childhood experiences with my grandparents, and as we and they got to know one another, it felt like "going home" to me in quite a different way than my feelings about the created Texas family network.

Professionally, I was also involved with tribal life. As I struggled to provide good outpatient clinical services to a four-county area, it became dramatically clear why the Indian population of 40 percent represented less than 10 percent of the clinic's caseload. Traditional psychotherapy could not be offered without building bridges between the cultures. The two socially conditioned worlds were not completely incompatible, but ways of meeting and assessing problems had to be found other than those based on the assumptions and expectations of white, middle-class professionals.

This seemed to be equally true if my staff and I were to serve the Black, Bohemian, Greek, and rural-poor communities, which comprised another 40 percent of the population. But it was particularly the half-dozen Indian tribes with whom I worked, played, and lived who amplified and vital-ized everything I had already learned as a professional:

That behavior makes sense when one sees through the eyes and feels through the perception of the behaver;

That people not only can, but will, help one another;

And that any help, to be useful, must be part of the social context of the person in distress.

I had no hesitancy about attending tribal meetings, because they paralleled my professional background and experience in working with church groups, neighborhood gatherings, PTA's, and civic clubs; it seemed perfectly natural. Since I was working with physicians and civil officials, I assumed I should also consult tribal leaders and medicine men. I began in each case to search out the rhythms of existing groups and the sources of natural, social, and supernatural powers that were available—and to relate my therapeutic endeavors to them, rather than isolating individuals from these mechanisms of support.

All of this experience, however, seemed to be in such contrast to the dogma and training espoused by fellow professionals that I became profoundly troubled. There seemed no way to communicate these ideas beyond my small community, where I was peripheral to the professional mainstream. While I was struggling to formulate my theories in ways that would make sense to the larger community of mental health personnel, I began to read snatches from the field of family therapy, with its emphasis on the eastern urban scene. When my two youngsters had left the nest, I decided to move yet again—this time to the east coast to find out for myself if the answers were there.

Just as I was emerging from the culture shock of the transplant from West to East, from rural to urban living arrangements—and while I was very much discouraged because there still seemed no way to communicate my ideas—Jay Haley, family therapy researcher and communications expert, arranged for Ross to present his work at the Philadelphia Child Guidance Clinic. Here was someone who certainly was dealing with the total social matrix rather than just the nuclear family. It was exciting to hear Ross speak about urban assemblies that had direct and real parallels to tribal meetings.

I was particularly struck by the image of the "social network," a term introduced by British anthropologists to describe social structures of intimacy and range comparable to families and clans, but not based on kinship alone. The term is best described by John Barnes, who first used it:

> Each person is, as it were, in touch with a number of other people, some of whom are directly in touch with each other and some of whom are not . . . I find it convenient to talk of a social field of this kind as a *network*. The image I have is of a net of points some of which are joined by lines. The points of the image are people, or sometimes groups, and the lines indicate which people interact with each other.*

In a very short time, Ross and I began to talk and to work together in the excitement of each finding another "medicine man" with whom to share and from whom to learn.

IN DEVELOPING THIS BOOK, we have tried to express our sense of what could be done with the concept of retribalization, as applied to the crises brought to the average urban clinic. It has seemed to us that urban dwellers need to rebuild or rediscover the kind of multiple resources and mutually supporting relationships that have been eroded away as city folk lost ties with clans, villages, and their own extended families. We have centered our discussions around crises

---

*"Class and Committees in a Norwegian Island Parish," *Human Relations,* Vol. 7, No. 1 (1954), p. 43.

because these are the easiest times to overcome the inertial effect of the depersonalizing, isolating, mythologized self-sufficiency that seems to permeate megalopolis: in times of crisis, both professionals and the nuclear family or group are motivated to muster the courage to round up all the significant people and to utilize their help. Crisis also tends to focus the efforts of the active helpers who emerge—and they do emerge in cities, just as they appear in small towns and among clans and tribes.

While we have used the term "tribe" as a frequent metaphor in our discussion, we find the descriptive designation "social network" more practical. It is not loaded with prior associations and definitions, so it is still vividly descriptive. A social network includes the nuclear family and all of the kin of every member. But it also includes the friends, neighbors, work associates, and significant helpers from churches, schools, social agencies, and institutions who are willing and able to take the risk of involvement. We feel that such a network of interrelated people, suitably organized along lines comfortable to its own culture, has within it the resources to develop creative solutions to the human predicaments of its members. Indeed we go a step further in our conviction that much, if not most, of the behaviors traditionally interpreted as symptoms of mental illness derive from the alienation of human beings from just these relationships and resources. Traditionally, the individual has been regarded as the "sick" one; more recently, the family has been identified as a "sick" unit. Our experience is that in some instances the entire social network causes and perpetuates pathology, scapegoating the individual and/or the family.

One essential difference between network assemblies of family, friends, neighbors, and kinfolk and other therapeutic group situations is the common experiential background of the network. Many network members know each other intimately and will continue to do so over time. They have a history of impinging on each other's lives. Privacy and confidentiality have quite different connotations and affective meanings in a group that shares a subculture and a mythology. The relationships in a network have a quality of regularity and dailiness, of intrusive excursions into one's past, present, and future.

Another difference between networks and artificial groups centers around the important function of man's primitive ritualizations marking birth, death, and marriage. These are replicated in attenuated form in the course of the normal lives of the network members. Assemblies of the network in everyday life can be fraught with guilt feelings, with rivalry, and with the perpetuation of secrets, collusions, and multiple anxieties. They are often uneasy celebrations. But they are real—not replications or role enactments in a laboratory or a consultation room. Social network intervention also deals with these realities as they occur, not with fantasies and replications. This is metaphorically communicated when the intervention team goes to the home rather than assuming that the network as a whole, will come to them.

When the intervention team assembles the tribe for therapeutic purposes, the accumulated past tensions are immediately available. This is in contrast to the intrapsychic ghosts who populate the atmosphere of other therapeutic modes, from analysis through psychodrama and the encounter. Most other groups in psychotherapy are composed of peers who are strangers. The members of an intervention team must have learned to work with procreative intergenerational units and their peers, who are not strangers to one another, and to deal with reality problems in all the complexity of daily social interactions.

This book is about retribalization through the assembly and creation of a viable social network for the person and family in distress. Our examples are drawn largely from work with schizophrenic persons, but we are quite sure that they have implications and applications for all kinds of people, in all kinds of situations. Particularly, we see the principles and techniques of social network intervention as useful for many different groups of people who have not been accustomed to seeking out psychotherapy. People living in communes and experimenting with new life styles, and members of many subcultures, may even be able to pick up from here and adapt preventive measures to keep their networks viable. We hope our ideas will help the professional take another look at youth, minority peoples, and other subcultures instead of shunting them aside as "unsuitable for treatment."

We hope we are sharing the authenticity of our own experience, and that this will break the ground for others to follow, to innovate, and to investigate—and that understanding the complexities and rhythms of the network effect will make it possible for many therapists to make their own adaptations. If psychotherapy is to evolve to meet the needs of today's world, everyone must participate fully in carrying the process of intervention on to the next stages of its development. We know that only when both the general public and the professional meet as equal partners can the best results be obtained.

Equally strong is our conviction that among the general readers of this book should be a number of activists who will recognize the potential of a partially functioning social network—perhaps in their church, community organization, or the dying-out tradition of a family reunion. We hope they will gain here a new appreciation of its value and an awareness of how, by recognizing and utilizing the network effect, they may revive and preserve these tribal resources before they are lost to those who so desperately need them.

We realize that a great deal must be lost in compressing

the network assembly process into print, and that many of the emotional currents we attempt to transmit can only be suggested to the imagination. But many professionals want a walk-through of the network assembly process, and those who have shared some of these retribalizing experiences with us are also sharing the pressure to teach and train others.

The first section that follows describes our own theory of how retribalization takes place in urban settings, and how it has been utilized in times of crisis in specific cases. We follow this with some detailed description of the phases in the network assembly process, and a transcription of a network assembly session.

An Appendix offers some information for practicing professionals about the problems and resources for team training—as well as some applications of these principles that have evolved in consultation with professional agencies and organizations.

Both of us are keeping in contact with our own tribal roots —Ross's stretch out and back to Canada and England, while Carolyn touches base in California, Texas, and Oklahoma and consults on various tribal and Indian projects. We have enjoyed being part of a network of network interventionists, and we expect it to grow and absorb new members among you. Our theories, goals, and techniques are not at all complete nor in their final form. We hope that by sticking our necks out and by taking some unconventional positions, we will encourage many others to take these same risks.

Ross V. Speck, Philadelphia, Pennsylvania
Carolyn L. Attneave, Brookline, Massachusetts

Family Networks

Prologue

IN PRESERVATION HALL in New Orleans, old black men from the early Dixieland era improvise and invent jazz nightly. The audience of habitués and tourists begins the evening relatively unrelated to one another, at separate tables and in couples or small groups. Under the mystical, religious, tribal, hypnotic, musical spell they become closely knitted together. They sit tightly pressed. The small group boundaries dissolve. They clap, sway, beat out rhythms, and move their bodies in a united complex response. The group mood is a euphoric "high," and the conventional binds dissolve. New relationships melt away the conventional barriers of status, generation, territory, and sex. Young middle-class white women, black street people, elderly spinsters, and hippie youths recognize a mutuality and express it in gesture, contact, and in words. This lasts until the musicians give out and the people depart. Many leave in groups they might never have contemplated before they came. For those brief hours they have become involved with one another and with humanity in general in new ways, with new feelings, new relationships, and new bonds. However briefly, they have been a part of a social network. They have experienced the network effect.

1

The Network Effect

EARLY IN OUR EXPERIENCES with social network intervention, we became aware of a phenomenon that seems appropriately called the network effect. Originally it was noted that a new process had been set in motion that had little to do with the intentions of the network intervenor. It was a bonus that in some ways made network intervention more fun and more interesting, but it seemed tangential to the goal-directed tasks of therapy. Further reflection and discussion, however, strongly suggest that perhaps this network effect accounts for much of the impact of the various types of network intervention, and that it is an essential characteristic of social behavior in a basic and fundamental way.

The process is difficult and elusive to describe, but examples of it are rampant on the contemporary and historical scene: religious revival meetings, tribal healing ceremonies, and alumni or "Big Game" celebrations are time-tested institutionalized instances; the Woodstock festival, peace marches, civil rights actions, and revolutionary militant-group meetings are more current examples. Although neither might like to admit it, some hope of achieving the network effect unites the Lions Club in the group singing climax to its regular meetings, and the most far-out imaginable rock group with their tribal photos as a trademark on their record albums. The network effect is a "turn-on" phenomenon of group interaction. Once people have made this initial change, they can never step into the same river of human relationships again.

When, during the attempted resolution of a crisis, this phenomenon is induced in a group made up of family, relatives, neighbors, and friends who have had varied countinuing contact with one another, a retribalization occurs. Attenuated relationships are revived, while symbiotic ties are loosened or severed. Latent interests are energized by newly appreciated talents, and newly expressed needs elicit the sharing of practical experience. Old ghosts are exorcized and locked doors are opened; zest and fun are rediscovered. The world shifts in its ominous trend toward depersonalization, dehumanization, and loneliness.

The social network is a relatively invisible, but at the same time a very real, structure in which an individual, nuclear family, or group is embedded. There are malfunctioning social networks as well as malfunctioning families and individuals. The retribalization goal of social network intervention attempts to deal with the entire structure by rendering the network visible and viable, and by attempting to restore its function. Thus the social network becomes the unit of treatment or intervention—it becomes the "patient" —and the success or failure of the therapy will require new modes of evaluation.

Earlier therapies were based on the assumption that normal growth was predictable, and that if it went awry, a process of readjustment and relearning could repair the damage. As professionals, therapists became very skilled at managing this task. Demand for their services increased as the institutions of society fell further behind the pace of change and stress. Inevitably, as the established social order has undergone greater and greater upheaval, the group therapies—from the conventional group to the nude marathon—have tried to keep apace of social change. Much that is viable and useful is still to be found in all of these modes of treatment.

In social network intervention, however, we are experimenting with the idea of setting in motion the forces of healing within the living social fabric of people whose distress has led society, and themselves, to label their behavior pathological. We find that the energies and talents of people can be focused to provide the essential supports, satisfactions, and controls for one another, and that these potentials are present in the social network of family, neighbors, friends, and associates of the person or family in distress. So far as we can tell, most people have some contact with at least 40 or 50 people who are willing to be assembled in a crisis. In such an assembly, tribal-like bonds can be created or revived not only to accomplish the tasks of therapeutic intervention for the current crisis, but to sustain and continue the process. The retribalization we have been cultivating is not, therefore, a denial of the realities of today by a literal return to some distant past, but a way of restoring a vital element of relationship and pattern that has been lost. The goal of network intervention is to utilize the power of the assembled network rapidly to shake up a rigidified system in order to allow changes to occur that the members of the system, with increased knowledge and insight into their predicaments, would wish to occur—and for which they are responsible.

We have found that the phenomenon we call the network effect can be induced in such a group assembled around a person or family in crisis. When skillfully harnessed and channeled, this group revives or creates a healthy social matrix, which then deals with the distress and the predicaments of its members far more efficiently, quickly, and enduringly than any outside professional can hope to do.

Perhaps a metaphor will help at this point. If the water in a deep pool represents the gelatinous binding and bonding between people, the widening ripples following the fall of a large rock are the visible network effects—changing the apparently solid surface and stirring the whole mass into new relationships. Counterripples collide as the waves reach boundaries or are drawn into eddies that preexisted, setting up theoretically never-ending patterns. More complex patterns can be achieved quickly by skipping the rocks off the surface, or by sending a boat across, or by opening a new channel. But unless something persistently stimulates the water, either by changing the boundaries or organizing new splashes, the pattern eventually subsides again, leaving the surface calm and the specific relationships realigned.

In our clinical experience we have discovered the equivalent of all of these phonomena and are evaluating the desirability of the permanent and transient changes that can be effected. For instance, in the case of one young schizophrenic girl who was symbiotically bound to her mother, activation of several network members broke through the usually reticent relationships enough for them to find her an apartment, physically move her into it, and support her through the initial phases of disorientation as the symbiotic bonds gave way to the development of a greater sense of self. The ripple effects were observed when the ringleader of this group, who had been unemployed for several months and was spending his time writing poetry, began to look for a job. In a matter of weeks, participation in the network had transformed him from a disheveled, bitter, depressed, and angry young man into a clean-cut business executive type with medium-long hair. (No value judgement intended.) Another member who had participated in breaking the index girl's symbiotic binds

temporarily separated from her husband, saying that she had
finally found the strength to stand up to him and renegotiate
the relationship. This example could be spun out to illustrate
the reactions that affected employment, marital, personal,
and interactional patterns in the lives of at least a dozen
members of the social network over the next six or eight
weeks.

It would seem that the network effect begins once members realize that they are now part of a special human cluster.
Therapeutic intervention labels this as a network, and works
within the newly formed associative groupings—tightening,
stimulating, and coalescing. The first sensation is a new feeling of freedom. There are fewer rules, at least fewer formal-
ized ones, in the new context. The network intervenors try
to keep alive this openness, this sense of new options, so that
the network members learn for themselves how to be innovative and creative. Learning is rapid as they discard rules that
do not work, or that are limiting, and begin to cherish a
certain looseness of regulation that potentiates freedom. This
sense of freedom, validated through shared intimate experience, is a "high," a euphoric experience that energizes the
group with confidence so that they can begin to tackle their
everyday problems. In part, their success is due to the fact
that their problems have been redefined by the new group
culture, which strips off old labels, collapses old roles, and
punctures old routines that are difficult to get out of.

Once we began to conceptualize in this way, we began to
get rid of the "sick" model for many patients. We also began
to get rid of the "healer" model for the therapist, and this left
us uneasy—particularly in figuring out how to collect fees for
an as-yet-undefined and largely intuitive service to a new
population. Tradition tells society what is acceptable by
defining what is sick. When called upon, most therapists
have then taken the sick person and told him he must become

like the majority, for which the system will reward him. What hasn't always been dealt with in practice, although realized in theory, is that the system needs a certain number of persons to scapegoat—to define as sick—in order to define itself. Thus if one person gets over his need to be scapegoated, he has to be replaced by someone else. The other alternative is for him to find that being sick is more fun, and to remain chronically ill. In either case, therapists are apt to find themselves in the middle of a cybernated pegboard game in which, if you press one peg, sometimes two or three more pop up. Most of the time only one pops up—but only occasionally, and apparently by chance, do no pop-ups occur.

The network effect can scramble the cybernated pegboard, open up new feedback connections, and make everybody both an experimenter and a validator of new options. Suddenly, *no one is sick.*

Network Intervention

A few terms need clarification in discussing therapeutic intervention.

NETWORK: A network is the total relational field of a person and usually has space/time representation. Although a network has a low degree of visibility, it has a high degree of information-exchange properties. A network has few formal rules, but consists of relationships between many persons, some of whom are known to many others in the network, while others merely form a linkage between persons —this linkage often being unknown to the two persons linked by the third. (A may know B, and B may know C, but B's common relationship to A and C may be unknown to both A and C.)

A network is much larger in size than most groups. Functionally, network size runs from a minimum of about 15 to upwards of 100 persons. Over time, networks are represented by the multigenerational extended family; while in contemporary space, networks are represented by family friends, peers, and neighbors. Any individual's network is the sum total of human relationships that have a lasting significance in his or her life. Networks allow for relative freedom of mobility, as compared to more fixed, codified, and regulated groups.

There are also "networks of networks," for which no better term than "tribes" presently suggests itself. These provide a meaning for many individuals through a chaining of relationships that gives a sense of identity and participation in a larger whole. Woodstock Nation was a tribal assembly encompassing many of the networks of the under-30 generation. The early Christian Church or the Communist Party Movement in various countries are other examples of tribal networks that have had meaning for many people over lengthy time spans. It is probably not at all accidental that the various minority groups seeking to emerge as potent forces today refer to their tribal associations for identity— whether among the Black, the Brown, or the Red. In so doing, they recognize the potency of the network effect for both individual and social change, as well as the vulnerability of the presently dominant White group, which finds it difficult to organize itself along tribal lines.

A tribe has a shared experience, accumulates a history, and encompasses both formal group rules and roles and informal, random collections of people with great efficiency. When it loses this resilience, it is no longer viable, and the induction of new members as well as the release of potentiating energy within the group slows down or ceases. The tribe may linger anachronistically as a kind of living fossil, or it may fragment itself and dissolve. Occasionally a network-

effect experience revives a fossilized tribe with a recombination of traditional and innovative functions and relationships.

Where such a recombination is perennially possible, a tribe
may persist over time spans of many generations. But where
polarities develop around changes, generation gaps appear,
and the social fabric appears rent with unbridgeable fissures
—much like the breaking up of the ice floes in northern seas.
Just as networks are made up of linkages between people,
some of which are focal, the tribe has linkages between its
member networks that enable it to transmit information with
rapidity and to mobilize efficiently.

When networks or tribes become stuck in reverberating
pathological processes, and many do, the members can be
helped better by network intervention than by the herding of
individuals and families into clinics.

INTERVENOR: An equivalent term for therapist, but
encompassing a new model rather than the old "healer"
model. The former "patient" is redefined as a person behaving in a maladaptive manner, which is both personally unsat-
isfying, and disruptive or disturbing to at least one group of
close family, friends, or associates. Instead of using pathology as an index, the intervenors are concerned with *degrees of distress* and predicaments.

NETWORK ACTIVISTS: Individuals who can mobilize
action and organize its execution.

FAMILY: Usually defined to include all the people in one
household, whether related by blood or not.

EXTENDED FAMILY: Designates the kinship system in
common usage and may include adoptive relationships,
whether legally and formally recognized or merely sanc-
tioned by custom and tradition.

NETWORK INTERVENTION TEAM: An association
of intervenors, usually professionals, but at times including

experienced network activists from other networks. They provide a cluster that multiplies impact on the network, validates and rectifies the experience shared by the intervenors, and assists in preventing the induction of intervenors into the network. Roles often evolve spontaneously as each team develops experience and are seldom formally differentiated.

The Therapeutic Intervention: Changing the Frame of Reference

The therapeutic intervention usually consists of: (1) Redefining the behavior first presented as the "symptoms" of a "patient," and describing it in terms of natural and orderly reactions to an inadequate social structure. (2) This predicament is presented to the daily associates of the "patient" and to a few close members of his network, usually his nuclear family or those with whom he lives in daily intimate contact. At this time the predicament is further defined into two or three specific issues that are potentially resolvable. (3) This close group is invited and encouraged to assemble its social network of friends, relatives, and neighbors, and to meet with the intervention team.

The techniques and theory of the intervention are dealt with in succeeding chapters. However, an example or two will illustrate how the professional and the family both shift their frames of reference.

Consider a case in its initial phases where decisions as to the strategy to be employed had not yet been made. A nuclear family consisting of a mother and father in their late 40's, a 25-year-old daughter, and an 18-year-old son came to the clinic for help following the son's acute psychotic episode —during which he thought his mind was being tape-

recorded and his thoughts played over the local radio sta-
tions. Jim also thought that the telephone system in the
house was monitored by outside wires, and he enlisted the
aid of his parents in tracing the wiring throughout the house
in a frantic effort to cut off this source of outside interference.
It was fascinating to learn that the sister worked at a local
radio station taping spot announcements and advertise-
ments. She resisted the initial efforts to involve her in any
family conferences.

At the first session with the whole family, an attempt was
made by the intervention team to find out just what kind of
help the family was looking for. Among the possibilities were
hospitalization for the son, psychotherapy for the whole
family conjointly, and the assembly of their loosely knit social network—with an attempt at network intervention by
our team. A potential goal in the minds of the team was the
mobilization of a supporting peer network that might enable
Jim to move out of the house and find employment and social
relationships more appropriate to his age and status. The
family was opposed to hospitalization, and at first resisted
family therapy by using the sister's work as an excuse—
claiming she would be unable to attend. They were intrigued
by, but frightened at, the thought of network intervention,
insisting that it would be impossible to assemble 40 persons
—the number we gave as the minimum that would be necessary. Jim began to assert himself at this point and expressed
reluctance to include his friends and peers in the same network as his parents' peers and kin.

The point of this anecdote is that a great deal of the
resistance to any form of therapy or intervention rests on the
lack of familiarity with it. Prospective participants are unable to conceptualize the processes and changes about to be
unleashed. Human beings universally resist change, and

those in distress are usually most defensive in the face of a choice about whether to introduce a new element or not. If they have never heard of network intervention, the vast majority of people will want to proceed cautiously.

In fact, both the intervenors and the family or focal group prefer as simple an intervention as feasible. However, where the simpler measures such as counseling, individual psychotherapy, group therapy, and family therapy have all been rejected, or where they seem inadequate to solve the family's predicaments, the potential network intervenor has to expand his or her own horizons and begin to formulate strategies around a new theoretical base. This is essential to get oneself into a network set. Once able to do this, it is not extraordinarily difficult to guide the family into thinking about themselves and their problems in network terms. We believe that this line of thinking does not involve any particularly difficult problems, but we underline the seemingly obvious fact that *unless one thinks in an altered frame of reference,* the likelihood of the intervenor being overwhelmed by the difficulties he perceives often prevents him from doing the obvious.

In another case, a 42-year-old mother had four children under school age. The oldest, a girl, was not presented as having any problems. The next, a three-year-old boy, was dramatically frightening everyone—mother, siblings, baby sitters, neighbors, and kin—by grabbing knives and threatening to kill them. He appeared to be trying to avenge his father's murder, which all the children and the mother had witnessed. The killing was the aftermath of a neighborhood quarrel, when the son of a neighbor, under the influence of drugs, invaded the family's home and stabbed the father in the presence of his family, who were watching a television program.

The third sibling was severely damaged from birth defects affecting his central nervous system and was quite hyperactive. The last sibling, born after the father's death, was mongoloid and was in need of corrective plastic surgery.

Although the mother was not overtly depressed, she was drained of energy coping with the four small children. She had moved from her previous home because of the overwhelming associations of loss and terror. She had lost contact with many of her old friends, and had no extended kin since she had grown up in foster homes. However, there were some foster sisters as potential network participants.

The usual rationales for intervention in a case of this sort involve the treatment of the mourning and loss, problems of mother and children, and the search for social agencies to relieve the mother of some of the more pressing and energy-draining responsibilities of caring for mentally defective children. If one followed the sick-and-needy-person model, it might be assumed that relieving the mother of her burdens meant either assuming them oneself or handing them on to professionals. However, a rapid assembly of the interested and able friends, neighbors, relatives, agency personnel, foster families of the past, and church-related persons of the present amounted to a large enough group to stimulate considerable change. Presented with the predicaments and given the responsibility to jointly participate in their solution, both mother and network members, under the stimulus of the network effect, generated some innovative and creative solutions, supported the control needed for the abreacting boy, and helped the mother not only to mourn but to find and form new relationships. The tribal unit of the social network accomplished all this in a much more efficient and self-perpetuating fashion than the conventional pattern of professional responsibility and patient dependence.

Some Thoughts about Human Social Systems

It seems clear today that at least some of us in the social
sciences have to become organized in our thinking about
behavior and the modification of behavior in large human
groups. In the McLuhan world of instant tribalization, each
of us is influenced by mass behaviors—from protests to festivals. All of us have been implicated, positively or negatively,
in the characteristics of what Abbie Hoffman has termed
"Woodstock Nation" and what Theodore Roszak has called
the "counter culture." This implies a polarization of
humanity—perhaps receding now—into youth and adults,
probably attributable to the fragmentation of social networks
that held past generations together with a sense of unity in
time and space.

Therapists need to be willing to begin to experiment with
and study these kinds of changing human-group phenomena,
which operate at levels that, during the past couple of centuries, have been thought of as political. Unless we do this, it
is questionable how relevant any kind of current therapy, or
indeed the social sciences in general, are going to be. The
culture is continuing to change so rapidly that the old methods of intervention with individuals, families, and groups
must change with it, or find themselves outdated and fossilized.

Social upheavals—in sexuality, in dress, in new kinds of
social relationships—create new tensions and precipitate distress that should not be interpreted as a new guise for old
pathologies. Clinically, adolescents seen today are simply not
the same as the youth of the past two or three generations.
They appear depressed and hopeless, but they admit it rather
than blame themselves. They see the world situation as hopeless, and they are hungry—but for dialogue, not therapy.
They are suffering from real distress of the soul, and so are

their parents, teachers, and peers. Intuitively, they sense something more than they can articulate about these upheavals.

If the psychotherapist is to maintain a healing relationship with human beings in this predicament—if he is to be of value in relieving distress—he has to innovate. As we began to do this ourselves, and as our colleagues began sharing their innovations, we found that new ideas are not always new. Ancient tribal wisdom is often relevant. What we hope to share is something of our understanding of what seems to make both the new and the old viable.

2

The Phases of the Network Effect

DURING THE COURSE of working with the network effect in therapeutic interventions, we have observed a recurring cycle of six distinct phases that occur as parts of the process. The cycle is not merely circular—in fact, circularity and the inability to move ahead may be the pathological process that explodes into crisis as tensions build within and between individuals who feel trapped. Instead, successful social network intervention seems to be based upon a spiraling effect that enables the group to renew itself: the experience of retribalization. The termination point for the intervention team is that peak of elation and exhaustion on the part of the total network where this renewal can be assumed to recur naturally. The activities up to that point of retribalization are designed both to capitalize on each characteristic phase of the network effect phenomenon, and to push events and activities through to the next phase until the cycle has gained its own momentum.

Although the discussion must of necessity be linear, it

An earlier version of this chapter was presented at a conference on "The Group as an Agent of Change" held at the University of West Virginia, April 2–3, 1971.

would be helpful now to visualize the six phases of the cycle in their progressive spiral succession:

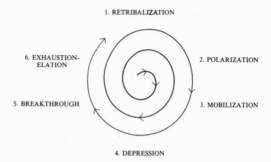

These phases are present regardless of the frequency or duration of the social network intervention, and even tend to repeat themselves in the microcosm of the single session. This is important to remember in planning network strategy where the intervenors may have only one network meeting in which to produce the network effect, as well as in the extended series of meetings that is more typical. If the network intervenor is aware of these regularly recurring phases, he can use the prevailing atmosphere of the individual session as a road map to let him know where he is at any particular moment, and how much farther he has to go in order to complete the work of that session. A knowledge of the phases provides him with cues as to whether he has to step up the pace or let things coast; getting stuck in one of the early stages prevents the full spread of the network effect.

For example, a network session may get stuck in the retribalization phase so that focusing and polarization do not occur effectively. The network may enjoy the retribalization phase so much that it is reluctant to move into the polarization and mobilization phases, which are the precursors of breakthrough. If a network meeting is stuck on an affective high in the retribalization phase, the intervenors must insist on polarization and mobilization, and then be prepared for an immediate depression. They must strive to get through this resistance and depression to the point of breakthrough, so that the task of the intervention can be accomplished. The elation that terminates each session can impart a forward momentum.

On other occasions, during one of the middle sessions of a series, the intervenor might have to deal with the depression that is a precursor of the breakthrough phase. At the same time, he must first supply, in a ritualistic and accelerated fashion, the opportunity for the network to go through the earlier phases of retribalization, polarization, and mobilization during this same evening. Then the most important task of working through the depression and resistance can occur so that the network will be ready for the next phase of the intervention at the next meeting.

Network strategy is planned between sessions by the network team. Options are always included in the strategies, so that the necessary tasks can be carried out with maximum efficiency and impact in a three-hour period. Flexibility in the use of various strategies is stressed in order to deal with possible emergency situations, should they arise, or potent resistances that render certain tactics ineffective. Whenever either of these occur, a new technique or strategy is employed to prevent bogging down to ensure that the full sequence is experienced. The techniques and the tasks vary in point of emphasis and amount of application, depending upon whether the intervenor is dealing with the early, the middle, or the terminal phases of the series of network meetings.

Phases in a Three-Session Assembled Network Intervention

The Jones family accepted network intervention as an alternative to hospitalization for their 18-year-old son, Claude, whose paranoid psychosis was aggravated and embellished by "shooting speed." Both friends and relatives of the parental generation, as well as friends of Claude, were to be invited to the network assembly. They were told that the team would like to have 50 or more network members invited, and that, in this form of intervention, there would be no professional confidentiality within the network. As standard practice, the family was told that there would be times when the process would seem strenuous, but that they must agree to meet for a specific number of network sessions. They were also told that if this or any other ground rule was to be changed, the change was to be negotiated with the intervenor. Forty friends and relatives took part in each of the three meetings, which were held in the Jones' home at two-week intervals. This account weaves together the six sequential phases characteristic of social network intervention.

SESSION I

Retribalization. The meetings were all held on Thursday evenings, with assembly time announced for 7:30 P.M. When large groups assemble, however, another half hour is required for the latecomers. Therefore, we did not start our meetings formally before 8:00 P.M., but the intervention team's activities with the family and arriving members facilitated the informal knitting together of the network. By the time there were approximately 50 people in the room (including team members and observers), noise and conversation levels were high. The retribalization process had been operative since the first telephone calls inviting the network to assemble. Old school friends who had not seen each other since high school days were greeting one another. Out-of-town cousins and other relatives were picking up skeins of family news. Fellow employees were meeting one another socially, and in a family context.

The formal session was now ready to begin, and the conductor took charge. His opening maneuver was to make use of what we generically call *nonverbals*. These procedures have similarities to sensitivity-encounter techniques and also have their counterparts in religious rituals, or the crowd and player rituals before the start of a football, baseball, or hockey game. They are like the warm-up phenomena for all performances, whether dramatic, musical, liturgical, athletic, or political.

With the Jones family network, the conductor first called for silence, and when he had some control of the group, asked everyone to stand up and put down everything in their hands. Then he gave them instructions to join him in vigorously jumping up and down, at the same time whooping and screaming as loud as they could. The other members of the team reinforced this instruction by example. The exercise was continued for three or four minutes until most persons were overbreathing and beginning to show exhaustion. At this point they were instructed to stop, join hands with their neighbors in a long snakelike coiled chain, and to begin to sway with their eyes closed.

The first exercise released tension rapidly, while the second one produced an almost hypnotic type of relaxation. During the swaying the group was instructed to say in one word what they were feeling. Typical responses were "drowsy," "relaxed," "tired," "seasick," and "groovy." This both reinforced the relaxation and brought about a group consciousness, which is part of the retribalization process.

While this was going on, the verbalization gave the conductor an idea of the group's resistance. As usually happens, there was some reluctance to group participation and to following the conductor's directions. In later sessions there was some recurrence of resistance, often more noticeable when new members joined the network during the retribalization phase of each meeting.

In the first session with the Jones family network, the conductor gave a talk for about ten minutes in which some explanation of network assembly phenomena and goals was presented. This was formulated in terms of the specific problems of the nuclear family so that there was a careful knitting together of theory with actual suggestions about what had to be accomplished by the assembled network, and how it might be done. In this network, preintervention investigation had established that Claude needed separation from the symbiotic attachments to his mother, father, and sister. It was also evident that his "speed-shooting" habit had to be broken, and that his lack of involvement in any plans for school or work were perpetuating both the symbiosis and the drug habit.

The conductor presented possible goals for handling the family predicament, but also stimulated the assembled network to begin their own formulation of what needed to be done and possible methods to achieve this.

The introductory talk laid out a blueprint encompassing all of the phases of the network intervention. For instance, the assembly was told that they would have to focus on specific issues; that the work at times would be difficult and fatiguing; that activists would have to come forward who were willing to carry out unique and innovative tasks; that complainers and laggards should consider replacing themselves in the network by other persons who had more energy and who would not give up until the tasks were completed.

The group was told that they would have to assemble for three evenings at two-week intervals.* They were also told that they would be expected to be at each session except for unusual or extenuating circumstances. This talk focused the retribalization on the crisis at hand while the network was in an affective, affiliative mood.

Polarization. The immediate next step is to find and activate the conflicting positions and points of view within the network.

The task of the conductor here is to apply some techniques that will tighten bonds within the network, using the affective high that should have been generated in the retribalization phase so that the assembled network will begin to increasingly focus on the problems that led to the intervention. One might say that this approach is as old as Hobbes, who stated, "The realization of the predicament is the precondition for liberty."

As the problem is defined, various members of the network choose up sides, more or less consciously. By allowing various subgroups to discuss the problem in the presence of the total network, the conductor is able to use the generation gap to polarize each group at times along dialectical lines, which can then be brought to a synthesis and immediately repolarized so that the entire assembled network is forced to deal with multiple levels of concepts and interpersonal relationships. This results in stimulation of the network effect in the entire assembly, as if large rocks were being heaved into a pool. The resounding splashes, intermingled with ripples, eddies, crosscurrents, and undertows are heard as the network members talk among themselves, convincing one an-

---

*There are plenty of exceptions where a shorter or longer series is suggested. However, a six-week series seems to be about optimal for the cycles to recur and the network effects to take hold in order to establish a retribalization that will sustain itself.

other, and increasing each member's awareness of the others.

The Jones family network had three subgroups composed of an inner, a middle, and an outer circle. The conductor asked the dozen 16- to 22-year-olds to form an inner circle on the floor and to tell something about themselves as well as to discuss what they knew of Claude and his problems. They provided a good deal of peer network support for him, but did not become particularly personal, even though several made allusions to youthful experimentation with drugs in general. It was not until John, a medical student in hip attire, began to tell of his use of drugs for pure pleasure that the rest of the youthful network talked about their own drug use. (John went unrecognized as a member of the intervention team throughout the whole first session. His youthful appearance suggested that he was a member of Claude's or his sister's peer group. Since no one asked, he and the team followed the usual policy of not telling.)

As the youthful group talked about their use of drugs, they became animated. They spilled out their views on the problems of young people, the state of the world, the war, the defects of the establishment, and the blind spots of their elders. During this discussion, the conductor refused to allow participation from the outside circles, telling these persons that their chance would come. The more the inner group presented a polarized position, the more intense the affect became in the middle and outer circles.

When it was their turn, the parental generation, seated on the comfortable furniture about the edges of the group, was asked to criticize what the inner youth circle had talked about. Universally they expressed shock at the revelation of drug use. Some became hot-tempered and chastised the young people. Most became actively involved, even surprising themselves. Again affect ran high—both within the talking subgroup and among the others. The spotlighted outer circle criticized and vehemently attacked youth values, "dope," the young people's attitudes about the war, and Claude himself.

For most of the early part of the session, Claude had remained aloof at the top of the stairway in his house. However, as the network effect began to build up, it spilled over the neat group boundaries, and exchanges developed between the youth and parental circles. As Claude gained in confidence and peer support, he rushed downstairs and sat directly behind the conductor, who at this point was seated on the floor in direct eye-to-eye, knee-to-knee contact with Claude's father.

Mr. Jones had become so involved in the polarization of the generation gap that he had come off his chair in the outer circle to challenge the youths on the floor. Immediately he became embroiled in a shouting match with Frank, one of Claude's close friends. The father became increasingly incensed at what he called "the lack of respect" he was getting from Frank. He finally screamed, "Get out of my house, you wise-assed young punk, and never come back!"

At this point Claude stood up and, dramatically pointing at Frank with one hand and at his father with the other, said, "That's me . . . that's my father! See what he always does!" This episode dramatized some of the family problems for the group, and as sympathies shifted toward Claude, a new polarization began to occur.

When this shifting polarization was sensed, the conductor asked the middle group to take the floor and discuss their reactions to both the older and younger groups. As anticipated, this middle group, aged 25 to 35, attempted a synthesis of the dialectics generated by the other two groupings. This natural tendency, which can be counted on to follow intense polarization, is the cue for the intervention team to move quickly to the support of the mobilization phase.

Mobilization. As the energy developed by polarization begins to become focused, it is time to mobilize and channel it constructively.

At this phase of the first session, tasks are often presented to the network. In the Jones' case, the meeting had been running for a couple of hours, and the network effect was well into operation. Intermittently during the earlier phases, the conductor had gently stimulated the activists in the network to look for tasks. Now the conductor suggested that three major areas needed the focus of attention of the network, and that suggestions would be welcome from the entire tribal assembly as to how these tasks could be implemented.

Depression. The conductor knows that the confrontation with a difficult task will meet with initial resistance, despair, and even desperation. However, in a group of this size there are always a few activists who will begin to attempt practical solutions to the problem. When a number of activists begin to attempt innovative solutions to a problem and to recruit others to join or support them, the depression is replaced by determined resignation and stubborn persistence to achieve a breakthrough.

To maximize opportunities for activists to reveal themselves, in the Jones' first network session, the conductor formed eight subgroups, each composed of six or seven persons. They were instructed to discuss the three tasks: 1) how to get Claude away from his family and living elsewhere; 2) how to get Claude off drugs; and 3) how to find employment for Claude. The conductor wanted a laser-beam type of confrontation centered on Claude. An additional focus on the family or other network issues would create multiple spotlights and detract from the combined network pressure to achieve a breakthrough for Claude.

Breakthrough. The network conductor must know how to transfer action from the network intervention team to the network itself. Each of the assembled small groups in this case was assigned the task of coming up with suggestions relating to three areas of Claude's life, and then reporting back, via a spokesman, at the second network session. Once the intervention team had gotten a group process going in the subgroups, they were able to leave the Jones' home quietly at about 10:30 P.M., content with the knowledge that the subgroups would run themselves for at least a couple of hours. (Breakthrough is the accomplishment of the assigned task for the intervention team, as well as for the network.) For the Jones family and its social network members, this first meeting broke up after 1:00 A.M.

Exhaustion-Elation. Breakthrough is followed by exhaustion-elation in the team and in the network. A natural recovery period then follows between the meetings, along with other ripples of the cycle.

SESSION II

In the first assembly of the Jones' network, emphasis developed on the phases of retribalization and polarization. Depression during that meeting was minimal, but between sessions it developed and deepened, so that the second assembly characteristically emphasized this phase of the overall cycle.

Retribalization. The intervention team arrived at the Jones home early, as usual, and suspected that the level of depression and resistance in the network had increased, as many members arrived as late as 8:00 and 8:30 P.M. In the meantime, the intervention team conversed with as many network members as possible in order to gather *Network News* to be presented as part of the strategy for this meeting. The conductor began the meeting by asking for silence, and used the same nonverbal techniques to reduce tension as in the first session.

Following this, the Network News provided an information exchange about what had been happening over the previous two weeks. This took the place of the conductor's talk during Session I. The headline story was that Mrs. Jones had discovered a spoon, some powder, a syringe, and a needle in Claude's room. Claude, even when confronted with the evidence, denied that he had been using any drugs and talked in a rambling and incoherent fashion from his perch at the top of the stairs. The retribalization phase was obviously briefer than in the first session, and the transition to polarization was almost immediate.

Polarization. The news session produced immediate polarization, and then the conductor formed an inner group composed of the seven spokesmen for the subgroups that had been established at the end of the previous formal session. Because of the high degree of affective involvement and polarization, the outer groups could not refrain from interrupting the spokesmen, and increasing irritation and chaos resulted.

This type of situation is a clear indication for a rapid shift in the network intervention strategy. In fact, the conductor may scrap previously made plans and, with the team, develop new strategies on the spot designed to break through the resistance and impasse.

Mobilization. There was an effort to move into mobilization by separating the two highly charged groups into different rooms. The effect, however, was to even further strengthen the polarizations. The resulting sense of impotence, frustration, and impasse deepened the premature depression. Both groups became angry, at themselves and at the other group, and exhibited open hostility toward the intervenors. A husband, in a tense moment, screamed at his wife for having her shoes off.

Depression. This phase really overlapped the preceding stages and was felt even before retribalization began. When the phases do not follow sequentially, the conductor must recycle the phase interventions in order to get the network back on the track. In this case, the whole network was reassembled, and a brief interlude of swaying took place. The conductor then pointed out to the group that they were depressed and stuck. This allowed a breather, after which the network could again turn to the conductor for direction.

At this point, the characteristic hopelessness and sense of facing an impasse require new energy and a more realistic focus of effort. It is quite usual for the first efforts of mobilization to be channeled down familiar paths, as obvious and simple solutions are put forward. But as the retribalization of the network continues, these failures are shared. The whole group experiences a sense of emotional impotence and begins to face up to the proportions of the problem that drove the family to ask for professional help.

From this shared depression, new bonds form in support of the troubled members. Moreover, some members of the network, not previously exhausted by intimate battles with the problem, and seeing it from varied perspectives, can now provide new ideas and new sources of energy. The respite offered by the intervenors in the form of verbal and nonverbal expressions of the network's feelings provided the opportunity to refocus the problem in an atmosphere of group support.

Breakthrough. The conductor quickly suggested that a committee, called the Claude Committee, be formed to deal with the issues that the majority of the spokesmen had suggested. Once mobilized, the network formed the committee and moved through the breakthrough phase in about two minutes. The committee, faced with immediate practical problems, began to function almost as it formed. A good mix of viewpoints led these frankly activist peers to both challenge and support the parents and allowed the total group to feel hopeful again.

Exhaustion-Elation. The network members headed for the refreshments in the kitchen in an animated fashion, exhausted, but also in a state of elation at their involvement in the new task. The intervention team departed forthwith in a similar state.

SESSION III

Retribalization. Ritualistic observance of the nonverbal activities and another installment of Network News quickly led the group through this phase.

Polarization. This time the inner group was composed of the Claude Committee. They had worked hard, and had come up with five job offers and three separate living arrangements for Claude. Two of the committee members had practically shut down their businesses in order to be with Claude constantly and prevent his use of drugs. They had also advanced him money to pay old drug debts.

By the third session, the committee realized that Claude was not cooperating and that he had no intention of moving, working, or getting off drugs. The committee, although feeling stuck and unable to reach their goals, had now decided to adopt a get-tough policy with Claude, which they intended to apply in the next two weeks.

Mobilization—Deferred. Meanwhile, the intervention team had decided that Claude's reluctance to change was being strongly reinforced by Mr. and Mrs. Jones and by his sister. Therefore, the team planned to spend most of the time in this session dealing with the rest of the family. They decided that since Claude had had much of the attention in the previous two sessions, they should force him to listen while the focus was put on the others. The team anticipated that Mr. and Mrs. Jones would be very resistant to having the focus of the session put on them, but counted on the shared experiences of the network for support in spite of the unexpectedness of the move.

Therefore, as soon as the Claude Committee reported, and before any discussion, the conductor designated Mr. and Mrs. Jones as the inner group and asked the rest of the network to act as the outer group. He then directed Mr. and Mrs. Jones to approach each other from opposite ends of the room, looking into each other's eyes, with silence and the expectation of physical contact. This was repeated three times with Mrs. Jones at first refusing each time, then getting panicky and attempting to run in the opposite direction, but finally submitting to an embrace from her husband.

The conductor spent over an hour trying to get Mr. and Mrs. Jones to talk to and about each other—about their lives and their relationship, independent of Claude. They protested that they had no particular problems, and that their only interest was in getting help for Claude. The other network members were also unable to make much impact on the couple, who kept apologizing to the network for being a burden upon them. When the conductor suggested that a committee be formed for the parents, both of them stated categorically that they wanted no such committee.

Depression. As the session progressed and the network saw the extent of the resistance, which included pleas by the Joneses not to interfere in their life situation, an increasing impasse occurred that was reflected in a heavy air of depression in the group.

Breakthrough. In order to resolve the impasse, the conductor insisted on the formation of a committee for Mr. and

Mrs. Jones, and the network reluctantly agreed. As a result, the Claude Committee remobilized itself more realistically. For the first time, during this part of the session, they realized for themselves that Claude was trapped in a mystifying* relationship with his parents, who were, in effect, encouraging him to maintain the status quo position even while they protested against it.

The establishment of the Parent Committee, even against the wishes of the Joneses, and the renewed vitality of the Claude Committee, allowed the network team to leave the third session weary but hopeful, and with a fair amount of satisfaction.

Termination. During the two weeks following the third session, the two committees were able to accomplish the three tasks for which the network had been assembled. Claude found a satisfactory job. He moved to an adjoining state and lived with relatives who had attended the network meetings. Away from his peer group, who were habitual users, and away from the frustrating family relationship, he no longer needed to use drugs.

Had it been necessary, the committees could have requested another session with the intervention team. However, as it turned out, retribalization had occurred to a sufficient degree that this was not needed. The three professionally conducted sessions carried the group through each phase of the cycle several times—dealing with each phase appropriately as it became the dominant one in its turn. Although termination of contact and formal assembly hardly means that healing is completed, or that all problems are erased forever, it does mean that the forces of healing and

---

*This term is used in the same sense as R.D. Laing has used it to describe certain communication patterns in schizophrenic families. Social psychiatry owes a debt to Dr. Laing, who first saw the relevance of Marx's concept of mystification to schizophrenic families.

strength within the group take over. As in nature, wounds heal and activity is restored.

Cycles and Recycles. The case example illustrates that an orderly sequence of the six phases was characteristic of each network session. It also provides the opportunity to note that the sequential emphasis runs longitudinally between sessions. In the first meeting, the major time and energy were spent on the first two phases, retribalization and polarization. In the second session, intense polarization led to mobilization. And in the third session, the depression was first intensified by adding new dimensions of concern, after which breakthrough and realistic retribalization followed.

This sequence of events is quite typical, and the need for cycling when the group gets stuck in a resistant or depressed phase requires that the intervenors be able to recognize where the group is, and what needs to be accomplished. The various reactions of anger, scapegoating, nonproductive efforts at solutions, and attempts to get the intervention team to take responsibility for solving the basic problems are all part of a depressive reaction that is cumulative throughout the series. It should be noted that retribalization, polarization, mobilization, and breakthrough are activity-oriented descriptions. The depression phase, on the other hand, is a mood brought on by the inability to cope in expected ways when one feels one ought to be able to cope, and manifests itself in a variety of behaviors.

To some extent, depression alternates with hope throughout the sequence. It occurs as the network effect is initiated and increases as soon as the network realizes (in the polarization phase) that the goals and tasks are not to be performed externally by the intervention team, but internally by the network group themselves. It reaches its peak when the volunteer activists realize that they have to mobilize in new ways and take hitherto unrecognized factors into account.

Furthermore, it is augmented when they realize that the intervention team is placing all the responsibility for further change upon them.

Thus, the depression phase is a recurrent and regularly occurring mood—a cumulative phenomenon that follows each of the first three phases. In a single dimensional scheme it has to be represented as a fourth phase at the time of its greatest depth (following polarization), when it requires the most attention from the intervention team. It is at this point that many of the subtle skills of the intervenors come into play, both in their ability to resist ploys meant to convince them to accept failure by the group (and thus to take on responsibility for change), and in solidifying the network's faith in its ability to cope realistically and effectively with the situations that have developed.

Breakthrough is the label for the relative absence of resistance and depression, and is accompanied by, or leads into, activity that accomplishes the goals of the network members. Minor or partial breakthroughs occur in each session, and recycling them is another task of the successful network intervention team. For example, in the third session of the Jones family network series, the mobilization of the Claude Committee, which had decided to take a tough stand with him, was deliberately delayed until after the shift in polarization to the parents in their eyeball-to-eyeball confrontation.

This started a completely new cycle without permitting the Claude Committee to get into action at that time. The temporarily blocked activity of the Claude Committee added further pressure to the network, which was attempting to form a second committee for the parents. The combination of this action on the part of the conductor, along with the parents' refusal and the associated visible demonstration of diffiulty in getting *them* to change, led to a buildup of involvement of the total network that might not have occurred otherwise. Without this recycling to bring out the additional factors in the situation, the premature mobilization of effort by the first committee would have led the network back into frustration, defeat, and greater depression.

Retribalization as a Realistic Goal

When breakthrough occurs so that there is support for all parts of the system, as well as shifts in behavior and life styles that remove the original crisis, there is an aura of satisfaction and elation. This is experienced as the product of the network's activities of and for itself, rather than as a piece of professional activity. The group has knit itself together into a kind of cohesive system as a result of shared experience, which makes real the retribalization symbolized by the non-verbal rituals with which the process began. Following the high point of breakthrough, there is a natural quiescent phase, joined with a feeling of satisfaction at what has been accomplished. This is like normal exhaustion and rest, not tinged with depression, and seems to be accompanied by feelings of confidence that new problems, when they arise, can be shared and dealt with.

The ripples and backwashes of the network intervention experience continue for a variable period of time after formal intervention is completed. This is not surprising since, although this discussion suggests that social network intervention begins and ends with a series of activities set off in group meetings, there is actually as much going on between sessions as during them. There is much telephoning, meeting of small clusters of concerned people, whether formally organized in committees or not, job seeking, apartment hunting, planned social affairs, and discussion of the application of network effect principles to the lives of other members of the group beyond those for whom it was originally assembled. Diffusion of the network effect almost always occurs over wide geographical distances, including renewal of contact with friends and relatives across continents and oceans.

Once this retribalization has occurred and has been reinforced by successful shared problem solving, normal occasions for group assemblies can often keep it alive. Many of the institutions and rituals of established cultures seem to have originally evolved to perform this function—religious revivals, bar mitzvahs, weddings, funerals, lodge meetings, family reunions—all occur in attenuated form in our present culture. Older tribal societies seem to have been organized around one or two retribalizations per year with longer periods of activity in anticipation of the event.

We are sure that the healing effect of these assemblies has to be renewed in order not to be lost. In the ideal case, the social network would itself establish some means of perpetuating the cycle after the intervention team has established the pattern. The group that becomes a social network thus becomes its own agent of needed change.

CHAPTER

3

Preparing for the Network Intervention

Selection of Appropriate Cases

SOCIAL NETWORK INTERVENTION is hardly the only set of therapeutic maneuvers a therapist needs. Every patient, family, or other group that walks into the consultation room need not, and probably should not, be offered social network intervention. In fact, anyone attempting to use social network intervention as a panacea would soon become trapped in a self-defeating hypocrisy of super-salesmanship. While all people live in a social setting and, we believe, have network relationships that might benefit from activation of their inherent potential, this may not be the most efficient, economical, or otherwise desirable way to ease their distress.

Experienced clinicians have established criteria for deciding rather quickly during initial contacts on the appropriate treatment modality out of those already known and practiced. Psychoanalysis benefits one kind of person, and behavior modification another. Individual psychotherapy, group psychotherapy, crisis intervention, pharmacological management—each has its rules of thumb and its intuitive guides by which patients, practitioners, and techniques are sorted out and matched. Even granting the large noncognitive element in such choices, at least some characteristics of the appropriate situation for applying the technique of social network intervention can be set down.

One summarizing category would be all patients for whom family therapy might be considered the treatment of choice. Out of these cases, a fairly high percentage could benefit from some form of network intervention. "Family" needs broad definition, however, or else other categories need to be included: communes, college fraternities and dorms, and single-person households (which the Office of Economic Opportunity defines as a family) are some examples. The parameters seem to be twofold: 1) strain and distress that can be mediated via relationships with other people, and 2) the availability of some social matrix, no matter how chaotic, pathological, or shadowy. These two elements seem to be definitive characteristics of appropriate cases for network intervention.

There is historical evidence in the evolution of the theory and techniques of social network intervention for another characteristic—crisis and desperation. Certainly the earliest efforts of most network interventionists involved last-ditch efforts—or to bend the metaphor slightly, their efforts had the desperate quality that comes "when the ox is in the ditch" already. This is still a good criterion, and one that has some justification, for it capitalizes on the pent-up emotional energy that can be released suddenly as the network effect implodes the system. A crisis state is clearly a desirable criterion for network assembly, though it probably need not always be present.

Certainly identifying, arousing, or heightening this sense of distress and offering its counterfoil of hope is part of the pre-network-session work. This frustration of the family or focal group provides some energy for breaking through the normal resistance to inviting 40 or 50 people into one's home to share one's misery—people to whom carefully and painfully guarded family secrets will be exposed. The prospects of institutionalization, unending entrapment, or physical danger to oneself or a loved one seem far more threatening than the public nature of network assembly, especially if there is hope that the intervention will lay to rest the ghosts for the future. To this degree, the crisis state is a self-selecting criterion; without it, neither the intervention team nor the focal group might be able to mobilize the necessary time and energy for the process.

Self-selection sometimes comes about in other interesting ways. In several instances, as the grapevine spread word through a community about the activities of the network intervention team, other people would call and request "a network." Such applicants have already moved at least part way through the resistance to the idea of their family and friends participating in the solution of their problems. However, the choice should still remain with the professional, and the presence of a social matrix and the intensity of distress must be weighed for each request, referral, or selection from a general group of cases.

Other factors to be taken into consideration are the more obvious ones of distance to be traveled by members of the network and the team, other demands on the professional's time, and the task of getting the family or focal group to invite 40 or 50 people at a given time for the process of assembling the network. It is almost always essential to communicate early to the family (as soon as the professional has introduced the network intervention option) that if they do not promptly accomplish this task, a referral for another type of therapeutic assistance will be made. If this is not done, the family on the fence will toy endlessly with the hope of persuading the professional to try some other tactic first, and a stalemate for any therapeutic maneuver is apt to develop.

An analogy can be made between the release of the network effect and the harnessed chain reaction of an atom bomb. While this may seem grandiose in some instances, nevertheless, this style of intervention is always in the big-gun cabinet of the clinician's armamentarium. It should not be aimed indiscriminately, but only utilized when the crisis and social elements combine to present the probability of a critical mass, and when the negative factors of possible reper-cussions and energy drain from the intervention team's re-serves are outweighed by the clinician's vision of rightness of fit and probable success.

The Team Members for Network Intervention

The assembly and creation of social networks is accom-plished by a team of intervenors. The plural noun is impor-tant, for it is doubtful if this type of intervention should, let alone could, be undertaken by one person working entirely alone. The first strategy, then, is the selection of a team.

Varying numbers of team members have been utilized, depending on the talents available and the needs of the par-ticular intervention. Probably five or six is somewhere near the upper limit for smoothness, and a minimum limit is three. A seasoned team of three, appropriately matched, can handle groups ranging in size from 40 to 140.

The team must contain at least one experienced person who is willing to assume leadership, has a plan of action, and maintains a commitment to see the process through to a solution. In practice, it has been common for this person to act as the conductor of the network assemblies. But this need not be the case, provided there are other experienced team members familiar with the techniques, and provided that both team and focal group are clear about where the final responsibility lies. For simplicity in discussion, it is assumed here that the typical situation will be as it was in the Jones family intervention: that the conductor and responsible team member are the same.

Preferably the team should contain not fewer than two or three people who know one another well enough to share considerable trust, and who are familiar with one another's styles of relating and of behaving in general. Division of roles and skills is important, but not preordained. One person skilled in large group situations and able easily to command the flow of attention and energy of a network, as well as to know when and how to turn it loose on itself, is usually designated as the team leader or conductor.

The members of the team should be involved as soon as the case is selected for intervention. In fact, ideally, the team should help gather the data, objective and subjective, that enters into the case selection decision. Evaluation of degrees and manifestations of distress, social-matrix involvement, and its pathology as well as potentiality, can all be better evaluated by a team than by an individual. Sharing in this introductory phase aids in team integration, and makes it easier to ensure the total team's familiarity with the clinical, historical, socio-economic, and cultural factors that will characterize the network.

While early total-team involvement may be an ideal that cannot always be realized, debriefing and strategy-planning sessions for the team are not luxuries and cannot be slighted. Data—cognitive and affective—need to be shared, role assignments implemented, and the whole team united in its conceptualization of the strategy of the intervention and its phases. This not only keeps morale high, but it provides for necessary response when network members call between sessions.

In order to be able to devote this time between sessions, as well as the "contact" time, team members should not have so many other responsibilities or such tight schedules that they become fatigued and strained by their participation in the network assemblies. Just as pacing and timing are important elements in the network intervention, the team needs to apply these same skills to their own total relationships and activities—in order to sustain themselves and each other.

The role of the conductor is somewhat like that of a good discussion leader or a good theatrical director (particularly if he or she knows the Stanislavsky techniques). A sense of timing, an empathy with emotional highlights, a sense of group moods and undercurrents, and some charismatic presence are all part of the equipment that is desirable. Along with the ability to command attention, the leader must have the confidence that comes with considerable experience in dealing with difficult situations and knowing human beings under stress.

Equally important, he should also have the ability to efface himself, to delegate responsibility emphatically and pointedly. Throughout the network intervention process, the professional aims to diffuse responsibility rather than collect it for himself. One neophyte team commented that, in their attempts at networks, the professionals did all the talking. By comparison, those sessions organized by experienced teams deceptively appear to run themselves after getting started. In fact, in several instances, teams have been known to leave at about 11 o'clock and have been told the next day that the remaining network members hadn't noticed their departure for at least an hour, and had kept right on talking for an hour after *that.*

The other team members should share at least some of the skills necessary for the conductor, but they may contribute special characteristics, as well. If the network includes a wide range of generations, for example, it is often helpful to have one young person and one grandparent type on the team so that mingling and participation by all members of the network is easier to elicit and support. Also, the suppression of manic, overanxious, or inopportune comments is easier if network members are all matched in appropriate fashion and status by a team member. And when the network divides into committees and subgroups, team members can be most helpful when they blend easily with them.

It might be pointed out here that if there are three or more team members, one will usually be selected as a scapegoat, and be telephoned or vilified whenever the network or any part of it is either angry at the leader or frustrated by its own impotence. This role might as well be anticipated, even though one cannot always predict before the first meeting whom the network will elect for this sacrificial position.

Because network interventions are still not common practice, and because they still tend to be most appropriately used in crisis situations and in a variety of settings, each team is put together on the spot, around an experienced conductor and one or two team members who have worked with other networks. Teams also usually include two, three, or more neophytes who have expressed interest in learning network intervention by apprenticeship. Their roles as both active participant and trainee should be given equal emphasis at the time of their designation as team members; otherwise, team morale will suffer from the extra burden of carrying dead weight in a situation that already stretches each member's capacity for relating and applying skills. By the time a team member has worked with the same team for about six interventions of three to six sessions each, he or she usually has an understanding of the process. Although this qualifies him as one of the experienced members of a nuclear team, it rarely means that these experienced team members are yet qualified or ready to act as conductors.

One important skill needed within the team is some familiarity with nonverbal encounter techniques and their impact on groups and individuals. The nonverbal reactions of the group are not only extremely sensitive cues and clues for the intervention team, but by building a nonverbal network experience, a ritual function takes place that sustains the network effect. The release of tension from jumping, shouting, or screaming, the calming effect of group swaying, the solidarity that comes from huddling and handclasping— all of these knot together the network in a way that meeting and talking cannot do alone. One often notes that if a pattern of nonverbal techniques has been utilized to open the first meeting, the network members feel uneasy if it is omitted at the next meeting. That newcomers or latecomers are most easily melted into the social setting via these techniques is almost self-evident if one observes the number of informal, nonverbal rituals that are part of common courtesy in everyday life. Notice in the next social gathering or committee meeting how latecomers are absorbed by members who offer chairs, move over, touch, exchange meaningful looks, etc.

Scattered through the crowd, the intervention team can respond to the leader's directions spontaneously and dramatically, catalyzing the contagion and drawing everyone into participation. If the dignified "doctor" is willing to take off his shoes and sit on the floor, or look at the ceiling and let out a rebel yell or a war whoop, or close his eyes and sway while the whole group watches, then it becomes safe for the wives and husbands, the kids and the parents, the relatives and the neighbors to do it, too. The team not only needs to encourage the participatory experience, but also, in its scattering, is able to release the more direct personal expression of feelings from those few who would not or could not join in.

Quick verbal and nonverbal exchanges of information are also facilitated by a team that is used to working together. The leader may need to know a piece of information, the content of a relationship, or the development of insight or resistance in some subsection of the network. When space and organization permit, brief team conferences facilitate this kind of flow. The leader can also utilize the team to verify impressions, check strategy, switch roles, or just let off steam. When conditions are too crowded, or the session activities do not permit team conferences, postural and body communications are crucial, and the ability to break in and toss the ball quickly and deftly about the team becomes more important. Network sessions last three or four hours, and leadership is strenuous. To keep optimally fresh, some spelling off of the conducting role, as well as changes of pace, are often useful.

The team is in many ways a miniaturized social network in itself, and its diverse activities and its faith in the intervention process is contagious. Teamwork by the professional intervenors is fundamental as a model for the network. This is easily confirmed if one observes the activists, who often adopt the bodily mannerisms of team members. The more passive members also learn that it is safe to fumble, to stick one's neck out, and to trust one another, as they observe the team and their own group in healthy, direct, open interaction.

In the first network session for the Jones family, described in the previous chapter, the youth group was most reluctant openly to discuss their attitudes and experiences with various drugs, until the matched youth member of the team spoke up frankly about his own experience and curiosity. In challenging a peer, they began to lose their generation-gap defenses.

Once this happened, they found that the older generation was both interested and attentive to their views. In fact, the tables turned and the older members of the network were amazed to find themselves feeling defensive about diet pills and tranquilizers. This was facilitated when the team members in the older subgroups insisted that the discussion was relevant and necessary. The leader was able to capitalize on the commonality demonstrated and shift the pressure away from stereotypes about drug addiction and onto the more pertinent family relationship involved.

As one develops a series of intervention experiences, it is often possible to spot certain activists, or even members of a nuclear family, who are such naturals at enhancing the network effect—especially between sessions—that they may well be invited to become team members for interventions in other networks. These individuals have often had spontaneous experience with network phenomena in their own life histories. And they communicate this experience both to network members and to the team in plain language, rather than professional jargon. This often has a salutary effect—helping the team members stay within the immediate frame of reference, keeping the team's actions and thinking oriented to the network itself, and to the importance of facilitating its activities, rather than taking over as professional persons responsible for all that transpires.

The team should also expect occasional phone calls from peripheral network members who are either timid or fearful about the intensity of the intervention process. Sometimes these persons call for help or advice with their personal family problems. Judgment about recycling these problems back into the network itself, or directing the person to an external source of help, is facilitated by team discussions and knowledge of both the intervention process and the characteristics of the particular network with which the person is involved.

In a typical ongoing network intervention, the team members can expect a total of 10 to 15 hours of work of this type between each session. When the method becomes more routine, with relatively stable teams whose efforts are mainly devoted to this approach, there will probably be a better utilization of time so that perhaps any given team might be able to work with five or six concurrent social network interventions. However, at the present time, most professionals cannot manage to participate in more than one such intervention at a time, in addition to their other duties. Even for the experienced team member, two or three may seem maximal because of other obligations.

Goals of the Intervention Team

Naturally the personality, physique, and aura of each individual denotes some of the limits of his or her role on the team. But their common goal is something else, and the team must be committed to it, regardless of their division of labor.

The goal that overarches all network intervention is to stimulate, reflect, and focus the potentials within the network to solve one another's problems. By strengthening bonds, loosening binds, opening new channels, facilitating new perceptions, activating latent strengths, and helping to damp out, ventilate, or excise pathology, the social network becomes the life-sustaining community within the social matrix of each individual. This does not happen if the intervenors act like therapists, since implicit in the therapeutic contract is the delegation of responsibility for healing to the therapist (even though, eventually, most therapies provide a terminal phase where responsibility for self is returned to the patient or family).

The intervention team must be on guard at every turn to deflect such attempts and keep the responsibility within the network itself. This means being able to live with one's own frustrated curiosity when the network activists gain enough confidence to take over. It means real, not false, confidence in network members who know the problems, landmarks, and terrain of the distressed person's life space. They must be free to do the thinking and acting that will evolve practical and efficient solutions. Since these solutions must be consistent with the life-style of the network, they are often unique to the specific case. It means the willingness of team members to be available to consult without being drawn in. This does not mean abdicating all responsibility—considerable clinical experience and intuition is often called for in making quick and decisive judgments. Basically, however, the intervention team must have a shared working philosophy of faith in human beings and satisfaction in seeing them rise to occasions, rather than faith in a professional mystique and a need to be central and depended upon. Experienced teams usually perceive that, were they so inclined, they could take any network that has been assembled, shift over to individual or family therapy, and keep themselves busy for the rest of their professional careers. For the network deals not only with the distress of the index person, but with the often newly surfacing distress of other individuals, families, and communities.

There is no other single goal—not cure, not treatment—but enabling people to cope and to share their strengths in coping, and also to reap enjoyments and pleasures that restore their potentials and set them up to handle the inevitable next crises of living. If this goal and faith is part of the fiber of the team, it is communicated to the network in a positive and responsible manner. Even suicidal and homicidal gestures can usu-

ally be controlled and handled by the network. The professional judgment that quickly evaluates both the gesture and
the strengths of the network is important. It takes a good
deal of acumen and experience to know when it is safe to say
to the family of a defiant, desperate person: "Leave him out
in the rain. When he gets wet, he will come in, and he ought
to find you drinking coffee in the kitchen, not hanging out
the window whining."

The network activists whose work during the Jones network intervention we described earlier exist in every network. It is they who, at the appropriate moment, perceive the
need for someone to take over temporarily—and in stepping
into the breach themselves, they require support from the
team. It takes guts on the part of a network committee of
activists to sit with parents round the clock while they let
their boy learn what it is like to earn his own living. It takes
compassion to invite a defensive, embattled couple to dinner,
a card party, or a style show, and make then comfortable
among guests and strangers. It takes reserves of patience to
find job after job for an inept, unwilling, and depressed person, and to help him succeed almost in spite of himself until
he finds out that he can amount to something in somebody's
eyes. Moveover, it takes considerable courage for most
professionals to turn these responsibilities over to someone
else who hasn't anything but his or her humanity, concern,
and horse sense to guide him through the traps professionals
know so well.

When these goals are clear, the skills needed by the team
are relatively simple to define: the ability to relate to people,
to sense group and subgroup moods and strengths, and to
facilitate, focus, and reflect back confidence. The particular
disciplines and techniques are raw materials, not prerequi-
sites. The intervention team will blend them with experience,
and use any and all of them when appropriate.

Sequences and Patterns

With experience, too, comes the sense of an order to the events that transpire, and a pattern falls into place. This makes it easier to work with the large numbers of people involved, and their subgroupings. It makes sense of the highs and lows, the ploys and counterploys, and the permutations behind the seemingly infinite changes each network rings on the organizational possibilities of human social relationships. While we have outlined the overall spiraling cycle of the phases that occur in the network intervention process, some subpatterns have yet to be identified and explored. It is part of the fascination of network study and intervention that there are still such unmapped vistas.

The opening session of a network assembly is usually one of a series, although on two occasions a single-session network assembly has been held. Subsequent follow-up in one case indicated that the network effect had productive results persisting for well over a year. Some interventionists argue that for therapeutic efficiency, the one-session intervention might be the ideal. But when a network has to be assembled, and the retribalization process started from scratch, more than one session is usually required. The experience of many religious groups, who rely on the network effect for conversion experiences, suggests that this potent force must be renewed periodically, or the group falls back into fragmentation and confusion. Intervenors need to be cognizant of such customs of renewal and, if possible, direct the energy of the network toward some such self-recharging cycle of its own, within whatever context seems appropriate to the group. While the first assembly of the network does accomplish many changes, the need for practice, learning, and insight indicates that a series of meetings is needed. The reinforcement that comes with shared experience tends to make the network a stabilized social unit that can continue to function without professional coaching. A series of six meetings (with the intervention team present) seems to be satisfying to all concerned, and allows time to work through each phase of the cycle. Sometimes three or four are adequate, if pacing and timing are carefully cued.

Keeping the theoretical model as a road map is important. The first session is usually one that ends on a high pitch of excitement and discovery. The depression phase has not yet been deeply experienced. The reality of the fact that the professionals are not going to take over at some point or another is not always clear to the network at this time; in fact, the illusion of professional protection and sanction may be very important in the early stages to free the members of the network to explore one another more spontaneously. Hope and communication are both characteristic of this period, with the retribalization and mobilization highs accented.

New team members often ask, "What do I do?" The answer is simple: Set an example of friendly interest, open communication, and unobtrusive returns of the ball whenever anyone moves to put the professional in charge. If asked, identify yourself by name, and if pressed, by occupation or professional role. If not asked, let people assume you are another member of the network—because for the next few weeks that is what you will become. Use whatever social skills seem appropriate. Establish human contact with as many people as possible—but also do a lot of listening and observing. Locate the refreshments, the bathrooms, the closets, the kitchen, the back door, the fans, the extra chairs, the ash trays, the telephone and its extensions. Help move furniture, if necessary. Get to know the people and the environment thoroughly as quickly as possible. If there are pets, identify them and their names and dispositions. Likewise, the children. Above all, don't get caught with the team standing grouped together and staring at the network members as if they were zoological specimens. Never seem to be talking at length about any interest that cannot be shared with part of the network—a practice as destructive of morale in the network as it is in daily life. In other words, team members are human beings who happen to be clinicians, joining with other people in search of a solution to a problem.

Be prepared for many anxieties and much fear at the first session. Very few people in the assembled network will have any clear idea why they are there. Many will be apprehensive about the distress of the people who invited them, about the risks they may be taking themselves, and about much that they have read, heard, and misinterpreted about psychotherapy. In fact, those who have had experience in marathons, groups, or individual therapy may be even more wary than the completely naïve. This anxiety has its function, since, as the session relieves it, the relaxation and confidence that follows is a potent reinforcement of the retribalization of the group. However, clinical skill and the ability to relieve unfounded fears and to focus feelings realistically can be important assets to team members as they work around the subgroups of the network in person-to-person style.

Once the group has gathered, the leader takes charge and begins inducing the network effect. There is a verbal-cognitive and a nonverbal side to this activity. He should introduce himself by presenting both an outline of the problems and an informal explanation of the network methodology. This is a brief sales pitch, and like many similar openings, has an impact beyond the cognitive level. The information conveyed to the network members here may not be as valuable as the sense of purpose and direction that gets communicated.

Immediately before or after this introduction, the leader

introduces the encounter-sensitivity techniques aimed at establishing relation and group consciousness. This rapidly inducts the network into what we have called a group high, where enthusiasm, activism, and polarization can break down the ordinary social barriers and defenses that isolated each network member prior to the assembly. A fight for control is often noted here, as the distressed person, his family, or a network member attempts not to participate. The team scattered through the group stimulates, initiates, and infectiously pulls the reluctant person into the group. During this prelude, the intervention team often establishes control not merely of the network, but through it, of the dissidents and distressed persons.

These nonverbal periods need not be long: three, five, or ten minues at most. But they do seem to begin the realignment of network bonds and binds. These nonverbal rituals should end with the group feeling solidified, in contact with one another, and quiet. At this point, the leader quickly forms a structure for dialogue and discussion that will develop the need for polarization. The introduction of nonverbal group-forming activities is an important test, which will determine whether the intervenors have the cooperation, interest, and participation of the network. If the response is halfhearted, the team must step up its tempo, and the number of nonverbal excercises must be increased. Participation by everyone must be demanded in a direct, confronting way until the group is involved, or the network effect process will not get off the ground.

In conducting a new session, the leader's sense of timing is crucial: he must have the ability to shift the tempo, adapt the rate of change, introduce themes, and provide the staccato and legato punctuation that builds to crescendos of maximum impact. As he introduces dialogue, the leader shifts the members' positions to form an appropriate grouping. The physical arrangements depend on the setting, which is usually the living room and dining room of an ordinary home. Frequently, people are seated on the floor as well as on chairs, sofas, and stairways.

One format that is adaptable to many such settings is the use of concentric circles. An inner circle of six to ten people is rapidly designated and asked to sit on the floor in the center. These are the more outgoing, often younger members, whose talk will stir up ripples and begin to polarize the group. Sometimes an outer group is easily designated without asking anyone to move, because the older, less immediately involved group has naturally seated themselves on the comfortable peripheral furniture. Sometimes there is a middle group interposed by the vagaries of seating and furniture arrangement. The middle group may serve as a buffer or mediator between the inner and outer groups, which will soon be polarized by the task assignments of the conductor. Often this group is midway in the generation gap as well, and interestingly enough, it is often the source of the activists who later take on key roles.

The leader not only selects the most communicative group first, but also arranges to polarize issues by dividing the network along generational lines, or in some other way dramatizing the tensions and differences he knows to exist from the preassembly process. He sets a topic relevant to the problem at hand, and asks the inner circle to discuss it among themselves in the presence and hearing of the total network. Once they have begun, he controls the outside group to prevent interruptions. This keeps the discussion focused, with everyone promised, and later given, their turn for interruption-free expression.

Often a fairly neutral, but subtly loaded, question is good for a kickoff. Like, "What do you think of John?" or "How many of you have used drugs?" or "What do you think is the basic problem in this family?" No one is allowed to escape from commentary, but no one is purposely embarrassed. Skill at giving the sanction for open expression is of paramount importance, but both leader and team need to be alert to support and protect individuals at the same time.

The purpose of the multiple circles is to produce more intense interaction among smaller subgroups of six to ten persons. The 40 or more members of the assembled network are too many for free discussion. Also, the multiple polarizations within each subgroup allow for the development and synthesis of various dialectics. It is important to elicit competitive polarities with diverse opinions, but only a few of these will be resolved at this first session. The wide range of topics discussed helps the network begin to select and focus on the major issues to be dealt with. Each subgroup is given its turn to interact with the other subgroups, and is instructed to listen carefully and not to interrupt. Later, each will have a chance to criticize what has been said by the other subgroups.

An empty chair in the inner circle is an excellent device to use when peripheral members exert pressure to be heard. If the group is large or intensely active, two empty spaces may be placed in the inner circle. Anyone not in the focal group may take the empty chair as a signal for a chance to speak. Having spoken, he or she is then obliged to return to the outer group and give way to someone else. Other devices of this nature are within the repertoire of every group leader or skilled teacher who uses discussion techniques. The important thing is to get the group talking openly to one another, rather than holding a Socratic dialogue with the professionals, or rehashing old arguments among themselves.

As the discussion gets several ideas on the floor, and some confrontations emerge, the focal group is shifted off the center stage and another group is brought forward before premature resolutions are frozen into the system. At first it appears that very little is being settled. This phase feels like a kind of brainstorming. The leader and team are setting the ground rules for widespread participation and much airing of opinions, suggestions, and ideas. The objective is to get out in the open misinformation that the group can correct, as well as information that the group can validate.

The network is informed from the start of the first session that there is a strict rule that within the group there will be no polite secrets. The team helps see to it that this is carried out. At first, the reverse of the usual professional ethic seems to shock everyone, but the network members recover as soon as they realize that they can trust both the group and the team. Network members often vividly express their relief at being able to speak openly about things they already had observed, but couldn't deal with in the usual social manner. "We knew you and John disagreed, but you would never let us help you before. . . ." "I was embarrassed after that night you drank too much at my house, because you never gave me a chance to say I felt the same way. . . ." "I was angry because you didn't let me know about Aunt Minnie's funeral for three months, so I didn't think you cared. . . ."

It is quite usual for people to think that their secret fears, foibles, and worries are concealed, even though they are patently obvious. It is also true that often people know only half-truths about one another, when the whole picture makes far better sense. But most heartening of all is the way in which people can not only "take it" when truths and secrets are shared, but also how, within a social network, the resources for supportive acceptance appear, along with a hard-headed approach to the things that need to be changed.

The sequence of polarizing, shifting, and refocusing—with everybody listening—is timed to end with a restatement of a specific problem around which the network can mobilize. At the end of the first session, buzz groups or a free-floating refreshment and visiting period are in order to take care of the exhaustion-elation phenomenon, and to keep the retribalization process active. Before breaking up for this, the leader designates the next time to meet and sets the assignment of a specific task-oriented topic. This is usually enough to get everyone talking, and as soon as that is assured, the team exits with minimal attention to goodbyes, beyond the bare amenities.

This sequence is a pretty standard format for the first network meeting, and is a skeleton outline for subsequent sessions. The techniques involved each time are selected in relation to the phase that is dominant and the context of the group and its setting. Each intervention team brings its own skill to the network assembly, and as it accrues more experience, it develops a repertoire of specific interventions.

Like all human beings, team members thrive on positive reinforcement, the most potent form of which is feedback information on successful achievement. For this reason alone, follow-up data is worth the effort and time expended to collect it.

As in any type of clinical and psychotherapeutic activity, securing this information is difficult and time-consuming, and complete information is probably impossible to obtain. This is complicated in social network intervention by the sheer numbers of persons, relationships, and goals involved. Another phenomenon is almost always observed: at the termination phase, when the activists have broken through and the network is standing on its own feet—elated and exhausted—there seems to be a sense of distance and a negative attitude toward the intervention team.

The negative reaction is probably similar to the sense of rejection and the resulting anger that occurs with each growth and development crisis in the life cycle, whether the occasion is weaning, entering or graduating from school, or retiring at the end of a career. Coupled with the loss of security and dependency is the sense of new safety after separation, which makes the former nurturing source a safe target for the projection of fears and hostility. A team needs to know in advance that this is a constant phenomenon, or it will interpret this backwash as a sign of failure.

In spite of this negative reaction, we have found that there is a residual store of goodwill derived from the team's participation in the network's shared experience. This rises to the surface after some time has elapsed, and is reinforced by genuine interest in the welfare and activities of network members. Follow-up inquiries after six months, or even twelve and eighteen months later, have often been more informative than immediate efforts within the first six to eight weeks.

During the course of the intervention, the debriefing and strategy-planning sessions are centered on feedback to and between team members, and are vital for team morale, and as a self-regulating check on effectiveness. These sessions also enable the team to get their bearings on the road map and to feel the security of knowing how far they have come and where they are headed. These sessions are essential for efficient intervention, and they also provide the raw material for validating theories objectively and for developing new hypotheses.

CHAPTER
4

Between Sessions

WE HAVE SHOWN how network intervention is conceptualized as a process initiated by the network effect which is induced by the intervention team upon the assembled tribe. Seen in this context, the intervention, or "therapy," is part of a total process aimed at overcoming the inertia within the network and enhancing the accumulating momentum of retribalization. As this happens, the network itself can get at the work of crisis resolution and healing, between sessions. This view emphasizes the intervenor's role as merely catalytic, and the network members' roles as central to the process of change. Because of this, it is obvious that many important events occur outside the presence of the team. The real work of the network goes on in the days following each assembled session. The purpose of this chapter is to trace out these important processes in some detail. The case example from Chapter 2, the Jones family network, will be used as illustration.

Between Sessions One and Two

The day after the first assembly of the Jones network, one of the intervention team members—not the conductor—received a telephone call from Mr. Jones. He complained that the meeting the night before had been too strenuous and frightening for his family, and asked that the next meeting be canceled.

We noted earlier that, as standard practice before networks are assembled, the family or focal group is told that there will be times when the process will seem strenuous, but that they have to agree to meet for a specific number of network sessions. They are also informed that if this or any other general rule is to be changed, the change must be negotiated with the team conductor. Instead, Mr. Jones tended to place one particular team member in a scapegoat role. He consistently telephoned him, badgering, complaining, nagging, and attempting to manipulate him (and through him, the team) as he did his own family. Until the very end of the intervention process, he avoided a direct approach to the one person actually authorized to change the situation.

While it is not always so overtly evident, the ambivalence of the family or focal group often expresses itself in similar efforts to avoid the change once the network effect begins to operate. They feel its effects keenly, and it is they who are often the most resistant to the surging upheaval set in motion.

In the two-week interval between the first meeting and the second, the tightening of the network was occurring in many ways. An interesting bit of evidence for this was the acceleration of telephone calls back and forth among members of the network—especially nonfamily members calling the Joneses. Several members of the network dropped in socially on the

Joneses for the first time in years. And several subgroups also planned a fishing expedition, as well as trips to New York and to the theater. Bonds were knit and reactivated in many ways as the network members developed contact with one another.

Meanwhile, Mrs. Jones discovered the syringe, needle, and white powder in Claude's room, which confirmed the team's suspicions of Claude's use of drugs. Mrs. Jones called the same team member her husband had selected as scapegoat and berated him for not already having ended Claude's drug-taking. With considerable feeling, she expressed disappointment that there had been no cure so far.

Claude himself threatened not to attend the next session. One of the younger members of the network, a friend of Claude's, called a team member when he found out that there had been a "narcotics agent" present at the first session. This was a complete surprise to the team. By calling the Joneses and some other network members, the team discovered that Mr. Jones had invited several business associates whom he knew were interested in drug problems. One of them was active in a Catholic youth organization that had informal affiliations with the police. Although this man was not a narcotics agent, the kids were sufficiently frightened that several dropped out of the next network meetings. When this man heard of the effect his presence had produced, he dropped out himself rather than intimidate the youths who had been using drugs, but who seemed to him to be trying to help Claude. This situation might have been handled without the loss of network members had the no-secret rule been successfully clarified, or had someone on the team picked up on the situation.

The team received feedback about much of what was happening within the network via Herb, who was a friend of one of the team members and who had originally referred the

Joneses for professional help, encouraging them to consider network intervention. It is very helpful for the team to have an intermediary who is a friend of both the team and the family or focal group. While this is not always possible, it does facilitate the retrieval of information about what is happening between sessions. Experience with many networks, and consistent efforts to retrieve this type of information, convince us that the sequential cycle of events and moods during the assembly sessions is mirrored in the activities of the network between sessions.

Because the major work of retribalization occurs during the weeks between assemblies, it is then that the significant developments take place not only within the family or focal group, but throughout the network. Eventually, these developments involve the activists, who rise to the various occasions and crises that present themselves. Mobilization by the network activists was occuring within the Jones network between the first and second meetings, even though it did not have a recognizable structure until the formation of the Claude Committee. Individuals and small subgroups were attempting to advise the parents, find jobs or educational programs for Claude, and were discussing various alternatives among themselves—occasionally contacting one or more members of the team with suggestions or questions.

During this retribalization phase, characteristic of the early stages of network intervention, there tends to be much confusion—not only among the network members, but also within the intervention team—about just what is happening, and whether or not anything significant will be accomplished. One apprentice team member has observed that the process for the team is to live through the same sequential cycle as the network, only one step ahead.

The team involved in the Jones family intervention met twice between the first and second sessions: first to discuss the initial assembly events, and a second time to share feedback from various parts of the network between sessions and to plot strategy for the second session. The techniques for moving quickly through the retribalization and polarization phases were decided upon, and the goal of activist mobilization and identification was selected as a team task.

Between Sessions Two and Three

The interval between the second and third sessions began the same way as the interval between the first two. Mr. Jones called the same team scapegoat and asserted again that the family was not going to have any more network meetings. He was again told that he would have to discuss this with the conductor, and again he neglected to do this. This behavior illustrates the tremendous inertia in the typical family or focal group—inertia that the assembly and mobilization of network members, and the unleashing of the network effect, attempts to overcome. This resistance to change is a very basic reason for attempting network intervention when other more conventional and simpler methods, such as individual therapy, family therapy, or even the inclusion of significant others, have failed to achieve therapeutic goals. The speed and energy mobilized in social work intervention produce a cumulative accelerator effect, while the professional judgments involved keep the energy harnessed and focused on the development of useful, rather than destructive and explosive, social processes.

The activists who formed the Claude Committee during the second session began regular meetings with Claude, and, almost immediately, one of them temporarily employed him to do errands in his office. The other members began calling their friends in hope of locating a more permanent job for him, while keeping an eye on his activities and discussing various plans with him for finding living quarters away from home, where he could be more independent of his family.

During the first week they lent him money and found half a dozen alternative jobs and living situations, none of which seemed to quite work out. Toward the end of this period, they began to find out that Claude was using their money to buy drugs and possibly to pay off old drug debts, and that he was either unwilling or unable to make any realistic moves toward independence.

Therapists frequently find themselves caught, at least partially, in such transferred dependencies. But in the concrete life situations faced by network activists, these impasses can be dealt with much more directly and efficiently. In this case, polarization and mobilization of the activists around these issues was rapid, as the Claude Committee increasingly realized that he was manipulating various members of the network, as well as his parents, and thus rendering them impotent either to change his life situation or to solve his immediate problems.

At the same time, through their close contact with him, the activists were exploring exactly what Claude would be capable of doing in a work situation, and getting realistic ideas of his strengths and interests, as well as of his limitations. The employment and living suggestions and plans became much more practical and were less tinged with idealistic projections of the activists' own ideals and dreams than they had been between the first and second sessions.

The committee was also engaged in attempts at negotiations with the parents, and a creeping realization penetrated throughout the network that the relationship between the Joneses and Claude was so locked in, so symbiotic, that neither could let go of the other. The momentum of the committee's involvement pushed them past the depression that hit much of the rest of the network at this time. It also strengthened the team's resolve to increase pressures on the family system in order to extricate Claude, even against his own will.

Just before the third session, Claude called an "emergency" meeting of the committee, which gave them a chance to act on their hard-won experience. The meeting greatly inconvenienced several committee members. One even left a wedding reception, and others set aside pressing personal affairs to meet with Claude at his request. Once they had assembled, he informed them that he needed $200 immediately because he was being threatened for having "burned" someone in a drug deal. By now the committee was onto him, and they told him that his calling them together was ridiculous. Not only would they not give him the money, but they made it clear that he would have to leave home and get a job.

The atmosphere was not one of complete rejection however. The committee offered to lend Claude $100—after he had earned $100 himself and could put it up as matching funds. With these assertions of reality and support, they left Claude with his family and returned to their own activities, hopeful that the parents now had a better model for dealing with Claude's manipulative demands.

Not all the action occurred within the Claude Committee between sessions, but the other contributions did not appear on the surface until after the third assembly of the network. Throughout this series, the activists were a phase ahead of most of the rest of the network. And all the members of the network were much further along in the cycle than the parents, and thus were able eventually to push and pull them through the necessary changes. Retribalization accelerated contacts throughout the network. At the request of the intervention team, several individual network members made estimates of the number of internetwork telephone calls during this two-week period. The resulting tallies varied from 200 to 600 calls, depending on how aware the informants were of interaction among the 40 network members. Information and personal reactions bouncing back and forth among the many network members, the parents, and Claude kept up the eddies and backwashes of the network effect. Much of this energy and potential for problem solving would have been damped out by the usual rules of privacy and confidentiality governing conventional intervention by professionals who assume responsibility for cure. The team was involved, but only in facilitating and consulting, not in curing.

During this interval, the team had several informal and formal meetings to discuss the large assembly session and the new strategies for the next one. As usual, various team members received telephone calls from both the family and the activists looking for advice and reassurance. A high proportion of these calls were obvious or subtle attempts to shift responsibility for the therapeutic work back to the professionals. This maneuver must be anticipated by the team and deflected consistently, since the ongoing life of the network must be sustained by the members themselves if retribalization is to occur. Experienced intervenors are an asset to the team at this stage of the process, when the demands of the network can create a team depression and much self-doubt.

After the Third Session

The morning after the third session there was the usual call from Mr. Jones, announcing that the network sessions would terminate. This time there was more distress in Mr. Jones' tone. In particular, he and his wife had objected to having the focus of the network session turned upon them as a couple. These two adults not only resented the new committee that had been formed to help them, independent of Claude's problems, but Mr. Jones reported that he had personally ordered them not to meet. The team left it up to the network and its activists to decide whether or not Mr. Jones' "orders" were to be followed. Actually, although the team had initially planned only three meetings, network members had asked for a fourth meeting during the depression phase.

Almost immediately a great deal of action centering around Claude began to occur in the network. Dropping his manipulative mode, Mr. Jones physically struck Claude because he had lost the key to the car. While this turmoil was going on, a cousin, one of Claude's peers from out of town, suggested that Claude come to his place. As the two boys left the house, Claude announced he would never return.

Five days later, Claude reappeared. His committee, well tuned in to the network grapevine, assembled almost immediately in the family living room. They emphatically insisted that since Claude had now moved out, he should find a place of his own to live rather than return home. Claude was incensed by this, but his parents leaned toward the committee decision, and he stalked out the front door.

The committee stayed with the parents to reassure them as well as to make certain that Claude did not come back. Claude's response was to pace up and down in front of the house for a couple of hours, periodically ringing the doorbell. The committee decided to allow Mrs. Jones to hand him some food, but stood firm in refusing to permit him to enter. Later ringings seemed more an effort to annoy, and eventually to anger, the parents and the committee.

The family became quite anxious and negotiated a telephone call or two to the team, in which they wondered if the police should be called. The team talked with the committee and backed their resolution to continue standing firm. Both the committee and the family were reassured that Claude was "just picketing," and should be ignored.

This climax occurred approximately five weeks after the first assembly of the Jones family network, and illustrates how the activists in a network often move through successive polarizations directly into the family or focal group, where the real breakthrough has to occur if the intervention is to be successful. They need the advice and support of the professional team, which often must make rather quick decisions. However, under the influence of the network effect, the activists can focus more energy, more attention, and more reality testing on the tasks to be done than any professional could possibly invest during such a comparatively short period of time.

For the next several nights, Claude slept in various places: on the floor of an office, and on the porches of committee members. He even went to one summer cottage offered him by the committee, but felt he couldn't stay because it had no heat. By the time he was ready to accept the committee's ground rules, they had developed realistic plans. An aunt and uncle in another state, who had participated in the assembly meetings, agreed that they would put him up in their home if he would baby-sit and assist at household chores in addition to finding a job. His parents agreed. Fully aware of Claude's pattern of behavior from their network participation, the aunt and uncle even resisted his manipulations in trying to get the use of their family car. Within a week in this new, strict, but nonmanipulative environment, Claude had found his own job, assisting an auto mechanic, and had settled into a fairly normal routine in the household. The committee kept in touch with one another, with Claude, and with his parents, but actively discouraged the parents and Claude from visiting one another.

Meanwhile, once this became a reality, Mr. and Mrs. Jones

were very distressed that Claude was no longer living with them. They made various maneuvers to restore the previous family state. For instance, they contacted a real estate agent and went looking for housing in the state where Claude was now living. They also emphatically refused to deal with the network committee that had been set up to help them establish a life independent of their relationship with their son and their roles as parents.

However, the knowledge of their needs could not be erased from the memories of network participants, nor could the expressions of personal concern be turned off. Telephone calls and visits continued. Numerous network members called the team to check out ideas they were about to try, or to report the impact of strategies they had put into effect. Although the Jones family had originally contracted for three sessions as a minimum, the network as a whole expected a fourth session, two weeks after the third. In its strategy-planning discussions, the team agreed to continue for a fourth session, and possibly longer if it appeared necessary. On the morning of the day of this scheduled fourth meeting, there was optimism among the activists that the primary goals had been achieved: Claude was off drugs, out of the house, and working.

This optimism was only partially shared by the team, who realized that a breakthrough had not yet been accomplished for the parents. Sure enough, around noon of the day set for the fourth session, Mr. Jones called the team member to whom he had been regularly ventilating his anxiety. And then, for the first time, he followed it up with a call to the conductor. Mr. Jones stated emphatically that he wanted no further network assembly sessions. The team, who had been in their strategy session when the calls came through, felt that Claude's new autonomy was shaky, and that the activists needed team encouragement if they were to persist in offering the help the parents were so stubbornly resisting.

Therefore, they talked to the committee about holding a network meeting without the parents, in some other place than the Jones' home. The activists of the two committees were at first pleased and willing to try this. But as they attempted to make the arrangements, they discovered that Mr. and Mrs. Jones had already informed so many of the network members that the session had been canceled that friends and relatives had made other plans for the evening. The session remained canceled, and the committees and the team settled back to see what would happen next.

It is only fair to add that the team was quite aware that during the holiday season coming up within the following ten days, the network members would be assembling naturally for social and religious festivals. There was ample evidence that the retribalization processes set in motion would continue. It was the team's expectation that these processes would sustain the parents until they made their own breakthrough. Sure enough, within two or three weeks Mr. and Mrs. Jones took a trip to the west coast together without either of their children, something they had never done in more than 20 years. This seemed ample evidence that the pressures within the network, and the Jones family itself, had so eased that no further team intervention was needed. Informal meetings and telephone communication to the team tapered off, except for occasional news reports or casual contacts.

Termination

The period after formal assemblies have ceased, until the team-network association has terminated, has similarities to the periods between sessions. Both are hard to describe because important activities are taking place within the network without a professional being present to observe them. The team sometimes feels like a theater company between the acts, wondering what the audience is saying during the intermission. One must interpolate thoughts and feelings from reports gathered unobtrusively, without being influenced or influential, and thus often missing much detail.

After the series of formal sessions has been completed, arrangements are usually made for one of a variety of possibilities for retribalization to continue, depending on the wishes and needs of the particular network. For instance, some networks have continued to meet weekly, biweekly, or monthly on their own. In these cases, the team, or at least some members of it, often agrees to function in a consultant capacity, conferring by telephone with activists, or attending small-group meetings around the current problems.

Occasionally arrangements are made at the final session for a meeting with the team in the future—a month or even three months after the scheduled sessions cease. This seems supportive to the network and offers the team a chance for feedback and closure. Very often the retribalization shows its effect in a revitalization of social functions within the network: picnics, dinners, swim parties, or group travel, as well as in the observance of holidays, anniversaries, and birthdays. If a newsletter has been started by the network, it will often continue to be circulated for months or even years as a means of keeping the scattered members in touch with one another.

What is important to note is that once the network effect is induced and channeled through its cycles, the network is able to run itself alone. The impressive feature of activities after termination is the informality of assembly and interchange among network members. This is so subtle that if one is looking for a formal ceremonial assembly to mark the new tribal feeling, it may be overlooked in its everyday guise. Indeed, memory plays strange tricks. While the experience has been intense, once the crisis has passed the role of the successful team is often forgotten. The assemblies that were part of the formal intervention are usually recollected by the network members with the elusive quality of a dream. Eventually, the realigned network becomes less chaotic and sustains itself with a more normal rhythm over the passage of time.

Whatever the basis for them, meetings of network members over the next few months following termination will tend to network "business" more directly and less self-consciously than during the assembled-meeting phase. However, if the network is to continue to remain retribalized, it will have to continue to have some type of large assembly at least once or twice a year. Often these meetings occur under the guise of a religious celebration, family reunion, or other self-perpetuating event.

It has certainly been our experience that once the tribe gets reestablished, they perform more vital and sustained functions for one another than could be provided by any professional therapist. Some of our greatest sources of satisfaction are the significant tides and eddies that occur within the network after the termination of professional contact.

5

A Single-Session Intervention

A COMBINATION OF FACTORS brought us to question the necessity for the prolonged period of time we had assumed necessary for successful network intervention. Pressure for time to see more cases made us reconsider our susceptibility to the arguments of network members for more time to learn, and for further sessions in which to obtain continuing support from the team. Were we only prolonging dependency? In addition, our own research interests and sense of pioneering achievement could hardly be adequate motivation for other professionals; if we were to interest colleagues in using network intervention, they had to find it practical as well as effective. Some contingent pressures within several cases also seemed to require a once-or-never effort if network intervention were to be successfully attempted. For instance, geographical distance may make assembly for a series of sessions too expensive in both time and money for some significant network members. Yet the impact of the network effect would be diluted if their participation were sporadic.

In theory, if the tribal relationships within the network have been attenuated but not lost, and if all the phases of the cycle could be developed in one meeting, then a single assembly might prove sufficient. While our evaluative criteria require further study and clarification, the results of our experience with single-session intervention seem worth sharing.

Single-Session Social Network Intervention in a Chronic Paranoid Psychosis

We were consulted by a young professional woman who was concerned about her 58-year-old widowed mother, confined in a state hospital for the past six months. This patient had shown a progressive paranoid disorganization and deterioration over the past two years. Earlier in life she had had about ten years of conventional psychotherapy for a severe obsessional neurosis. Always an extremely dependent and complaining type of person, she had worked most of her adult life as an accountant. Because of the daughter's guilt at having to place her mother in a state hospital, and also partially because of the symbiotic relationship between these two women, the daughter sought network intervention as a way to develop alternatives to state hospitalization for the mother.

After interviewing the daughter on two occasions, arrangements were made for a joint interview with the mother and daughter. The mother was found to be an extremely constricted, paranoid, delusional woman who kept repetitiously asking that she be allowed to leave the hospital. At the same time, she was extremely suspicious about the psychiatrist, about the dictaphone in his office, and about the telephone wires. She muttered in an incoherent fashion about the Mafia and about a plot to murder her. She became quite agitated when she had to leave the office to return to the hospital: she fell on her knees pleading to be saved, at the same time wondering if the team were part of her gang of prosecutors.

The clinical impression following this interview was that the paranoid psychosis might have an organic basis, most likely a senile brain disease. This clinical impression has not been confirmed or refuted, however.

The daughter was instructed to make a list of all the significant persons in her own and in her mother's life. She was to include all relatives both near and distant (geographically as well as in degree of intimacy) and all close friends and neighbors who had been at one time or other deeply involved in their lives. She was then instructed to telephone these persons and invite them to a meeting at which Mrs. B., her mother, would be present. The purpose of the meeting was to discuss among all the assembled interested persons the possibilities of getting Mrs. B. out of the state hospital, and of replanning and redirecting her life. Participants were to be prepared to discuss their ideas and to make suggestions. The daughter explained that several close cousins lived in such places as Rome, London, Chicago, New York, Texas, and Washington, D.C. We strongly urged that as many of these persons as possible should plan to come to this network meeting, which would be held two weeks in the future. The visitors were instructed to arrive in time for the meeting, and to make it the primary purpose of the visit. The meeting was held in the home of Mrs. B.'s brother and sister-in-law.

On the evening of the meeting, the team arrived about 45 minutes prior to the appointed time. Four or five network persons were already there. Over the next hour, more clan members arrived, and telephone calls notified the assembled group that the out-of-town members were at the train station and were catching a cab. A general air of increasing excitement prevailed. In all, about 50 persons arrived, including every one of the out-of-town network members who had been invited. There were about equal numbers of friends and kin in the group, and about twice as many were peripheral as had been in close contact with Mrs. B. over the last five years.

Mrs. B. took the team around, introducing us to all of her friends and relatives. It was interesting to note the affection and support given to Mrs. B. by relatives and friends who lived at a distance, and who had not seen her in months or years. This was in marked contrast to the attitudes of the immediate nuclear family and other relatives who had struggled with her as she became increasingly delusional and paranoid. The enthusiasm of the people who saw her in a positive light produced a marked impact upon Mrs. B. The people intimately associated with her most recently, however, were very caustic in their remarks to her, and spoke sharply. Her response in return was similar sharpness, bitterness, and paranoid projections.

Retribalization had already begun with the invitations to attend, and the greeting process was focused and reinforced with gentle group swaying, followed by the usual introductory talk about why people were assembled and the purposes of a social network meeting.

Polarization was almost immediate. The social network was split into two fragments from the beginning of its assembly. The inner group more closely related both in time and space had given up on Mrs. B. and regarded her in a frustrated, helpless, hopeless, derisive fashion. The outer layer of the network—those who had known her in the past and from long distances—still saw her as the wonderful person they had once known.

During this phase, many suggestions were made by the outer group, some helpful and some naïve. Several persons said they could not see how Mrs. B. had changed in any way, even though she had been in various psychiatric institutions and had been hospitalized continuously for the past six months. They refused even to recognize her delusional and paranoid ideas. They tended to see this behavior as her defensive reaction to the strong attacks she had received from her intimate associates.

As soon as it was clear that polarization was well under way, the team shifted to mobilization tactics. The assembled network was given the task of thinking about how to remove Mrs. B. from the state hospital and set up a living arrangement for her that would meet both her needs and those of friends, neighbors, and relatives with whom she would associate.

After about an hour and ten minutes of discussion, during which the meeting became heated, the conductor chose a moment to call for a break. With 50 persons confined to a small living room and dining room, this of course meant that small subgroupings would immediately form and that activity comparable to between-session contacts would take place. Although some persons wanted to serve coffee, the conductor felt that this would decrease the tension and facilitate conventional social patterns. After about 20 minutes of animated conversation in small clusters, a group of about ten persons was handpicked by the intervenors. Selection was based on their strong involvement in the network intervention process and their differing points of view and sharp polarities. This group was seated on an inner circle of chairs. (Most of the group was in the 50 to 80 age range, so the use of the floor was not practical.) The remaining outer group was told to listen carefully, but not to interfere, and to leave the discussion up to the inner group. If someone in the outer group felt he had to speak, a consultant's chair was provided where he could come and sit in the inner group while he said what he had to say. He then had to leave and rejoin the outer group. One of the team was assigned the full-time task of attempting to keep Mrs. B. from domineering and taking over the entire meeting. She had difficulty realizing that this occasion was not a celebration of her release from the hospital, but she also experienced recurrent bouts of suspicion, and was unable to participate in a give-and-take discussion.

The outcome of the interaction between the inner and outer groups was the formulation of a plan with two major parts. Despite the skepticism of the immediate family and close friends, most of whom felt pessimisitic about Mrs. B.'s chances outside the hospital, the group as a whole agreed to share responsibility for her care by a series of visits around the geographical perimeter of the network for a week or so at a time. The local network members then agreed to do their share by forming a committee to rent an apartment for Mrs. B., find her a companion, handle her business affairs, and plan meaningful social engagements for her.

Mrs. B. showed her usual distrust of the local group by demanding and getting agreement from the group that she be allowed to choose the committee and to have her attorney as a member. This committee requested continuing consultation with the intervention team, and one of the three team members was designated to carry out this function. Her role was to be available for telephone consultation and to attend occasional committee meetings to discuss problems with them. The meeting terminated with a high affective tone on the part of the participants and exhaustion on the part of the team.

Postsession Activities

The day after the meeting, Mrs. B. left for New York with one of her overseas nieces. A few days later, although phobic about airplanes, she flew for the first time in her life to a distant city, where she spent the next week with another niece. Then she traveled again and spent the next two weeks with other relatives.

Meanwhile, the local committee carried out their tasks so that when Mrs. B. returned from her month's travel, she went directly to a newly leased apartment, with a hired companion, and began her independent living. A series of social events such as dinner parties, shopping expeditions, trips to garden shows, and the like enabled the formerly burned-out and hostile sectors of the immediate network to develop positive interpersonal bonds from successful shared experiences. These occasions were important in order to give the companion time off, as well as to sustain Mrs. B.'s contacts with the local group.

It was not all smooth sailing, but the network members shared their problems and their own emotional reactions to Mrs. B.'s pathological behavior (paranoid accusations, compulsive ruminations and activities, and hallucinations). This open communication increased the bonds within the network and enabled them to cope more effectively and to accept their failures realistically. It was a new and valued experience for them not to have to mask either their fear and disgust, or their desire to be helpful, warm, and giving.

As we had anticipated, Mrs. B. had a more difficult time in adjusting once she returned to her home town. In the beginning, her behavior was manageable and within acceptable social limits. After several months, however, her extreme demands and bizarre behavior increased to the point where she had to be rehospitalized. This could have been interpreted as failure in terms of a "cure," but the goals of the team were in terms of the daughter and the network itself. Despite the failure of the intervention to achieve lasting results for Mrs. B., it had achieved its primary goal of initiating healing processes in the social network.

Over the next year and a half, a number of changes were readily observable in the network. The daughter married a few months after her mother's rehospitalization. The only son was able to drop his belligerent stance and interact in a friendly and more maturely intimate fashion with his family and friends. The striking amount of guilt-ridden and scapegoating behavior in the network underwent a noticeable modification. One manifestation of this was the friendlier relationships between members of the inner and outer sectors of the network. One key sister-in-law was able to go with her family for a vacation for the first time in years without any feelings of guilt over deserting Mrs. B. Many other network members reported a marked feeling of ease about the situation. Everyone had done as much as they could to try to find alternative solutions for Mrs. B., and the retribalization of the network enabled its members to go on about their lives in a more healthy fashion.

Evaluation of Social Network Effectiveness

In the more conventional one-to-one and group psychotherapies, success or failure is measured in terms of the end result for the designated patient. Often the medical model is used in which the patient is "sick" and must be "cured." This model ignores the growing contemporary viewpoint that stresses a series of psychological, sociological, and cultural adaptations that an individual has to make over the life cycle to be a functioning member of society. These adaptations may fail by virtue of inadequate adjustments at earlier stages, as well as because of refusals or deliberate noncompliance. In this case, there was the possibility that Mrs. B. had an organic disorder in the form of a senile brain disease. Instead of blighting the lives of her children and friends, this situation was faced and eventually accepted in a mutually supportive atmosphere.

6

A Transcription of a Network Assembly Session

THE FAMILY

Lena Levin *A 21-year-old woman who, in other contexts, would be designated as the "patient"*
Benjamin Levin *Her father*
Ruth Levin *Her mother*
Lisa Levin *Her 18-year-old sister (away at boarding school)*

THE REST OF THE NETWORK

Stanley Levin *Benjamin's brother*
Annie *Stanley's wife*
Elsie *Stanley and Annie's daughter*

Joshua *Proprietor of a general dry goods store*
Susan *His wife*
Rita *Their daughter*

"Doc" *The oldest established G.P. in town, who presided over many of their births*

Leckner *Another doctor, a neighbor*
Louise *His wife, a close friend of Ruth*
Sara *Their daughter*

Dora *Ruth's cousin*

Jacob *A local businessman, a friend of Ben*

Kenneth *A local teacher*

Larry *A young lawyer*

Several other doctors, lawyers, a judge, a number of young people of both sexes, and assorted neighbors, friends, and relatives.

THE INTERVENTION TEAM

Ross Speck, M.D.   *The conductor*
Uri Rueveni, Ph.D.   *The co-conductor*
Janet   *An activist from a previously assembled network in another town*
Four other professionals—a social worker, a psychiatrist, a psychologist, and a medical student—who mix with the network members and give feedback to the team conductors, but who are not heard as individuals in this transcription.

The Levin Family—Third Network Assembly

The time is late spring, too mild for a fire in the fireplace and too cold for all the windows to be open or the patio to be tempting. This family is comfortably wealthy and lives in a small town only now becoming suburban, rather an independent community. They and their friends take such things as country clubs, family swimming pools, and college and finishing schools for granted. Benjamin, the father, owns a small factory and its wholesale outlets, while a brother, Stanley, handles its retail outlet. Many people are dependent on the Levins for their livelihood—directly, as employees, or indirectly, in providing professional and business services to the people who work for them. Ben has had several heart attacks in recent years (he is in his mid-50's) and has an anxious air about him, as if responsibilities weigh him down.

Ruth Levin, his wife, is a member of the social set. Her time has been absorbed in charity fund-raising benefits, which she manages well, hostessing and attending parties and golf tournaments, as well as managing her responsibilities as wife and mother to the two girls. Lisa, who is 18, is away at a girls' school, where she is in her senior year, and is not present for this assembly. She has been sent off to school only in the last couple of years as things have become

increasingly difficult with 21-year-old Lena, for whose benefit the network has assembled.

Lena has been withdrawing more and more into her shell,
not going out of her room for days, and often appearing
disheveled and apathetic. She has been having some delu-
sions, with marked paranoid trends, and more and more
frequently explodes into violent rages. There is no economic
need for her to work, but the family has a strong feeling that
if she isn't in school, it would be good for her to do so. She
dropped out of college during her freshman year, when she
was 19. Her behavior has become impossible to hide under
a happy family façade, and she has not improved in spite of
efforts at individual therapy and at least one strong effort at
family counseling. The family, faced with the real possibility
that she might harm herself or others, but also frightened
and ashamed of the stigma of hospitalization, has gathered
up its courage to try social network intervention as a possible
solution.

The assembled network is composed of relatives and extended family from the town and points close enough for
traveling one evening a week, as well as business friends of
the family—including local judges, attorneys, the family's
general practitioner, and several other physicians. These people are neighbors, club members, and golfing partners, for
the most part, although a few are living on a more modest
scale than the Levins and feel a little uneasy in the unaccus-
tomed intimacy of this gathering. All of them are known to
one another in their various roles of everyday life, even
though they are not all in the same social set.

About one-fifth of the group is under 25—friends of Lisa
and Lena, mostly by virtue of being sons and daughters of
parental acquaintances. About three-fifths of the network is
over 45—friends and associates of the parents. There are also
a few representatives of an even more elderly generation, one

or two of whom are in their late 70's or early 80's. They do not participate much, but their presence is felt. Because it is a monied group, some of the network is away on trips nearly every week. And there are relatives and friends of the parents who live in a distant state, but who are kept in touch with developments in the network by telephone and letter. They are known to everybody in the inner circles, and often take an active interest by making suggestions and talking with a number of network members between sessions. A Dallas branch of the family is especially active, and became very involved in some of the later maneuvers of Lena and the network.

The setting for the meetings is the living room of the Levin home—a large room with a fireplace in the center of one wall. Two sofas that ordinarily flank the fireplace are pushed back, and the coffee table is placed in front of the fireplace to hold the tape recorder. To the left are some comfortable chairs; beyond them is an archway leading to a dining room where drinks and snacks are set out. In the beginning, some people drift toward this area as they circulate and talk to one another. As the network begins to settle down, some division of camps is signified by the clustering of the physicians and lawyers on this side of the room, and by their tendency to voice opposition to the professional team.

To the right of the fireplace are more chairs and an archway into the reception hall, which is fairly large. Ruth and Ben tend to be on this side, which enables them to play host and hostess as people arrive. They finally settle on a sofa to the right of the network intervenors. Although the rugs are soft and deep, and there are cushions, the age of the group does not lend itself to much sitting on the floor. A small knot of the sons and daughters, however, do sit on the floor near the middle of the room. Folding chairs have been borrowed for use when the dining room chairs and the regular living room furniture are all occupied.

Ross arrives about half an hour before the meeting is scheduled to begin; he has two team members with him. One is a mature professional who is observing and learning about the network process, and who drifts off to the dining room to mingle with people there. The other is Janet, about 24, who was the focus of another network intervention about a year earlier, in another town. She is tall, slim, and her dark hair falls partly over her face much of the time. However, she smiles at people from behind it, and her movements are only slightly stiff and embarrassed. Her problems were very similar to Lena's, but it was part of her delusional system that if she only had a family with money and nice, comfortable things, she wouldn't have any problems. In her family, her economic contribution was really needed, and work wasn't just the "proper" thing to do. The parallels in the present situation are not lost on her, although she does not verbalize them. Janet helps set up the tape recorder, and then drifts off with two other team members about her own age—a young social worker and a medical student. They participate in small talk with the younger set, and settle down with them in front of the picture window.

Uri arrives in haste. He is active, with a European accent, and is skilled in encounter techniques. His manner contrasts with that of Ross, who is taller and larger than most people here, and who speaks bluntly but softly. Ross does not need to use belligerence to get attention, and his gentleness at times is quite disarming; but one is aware of his strength and his power. Uri, on the other hand, raises his voice and moves abruptly, develops confrontations, and outbarks his opposition when he feels he needs to get control. The two are like a team composed of a St. Bernard and a terrier, and they share the tasks of conducting the session, which begins as people arrive and scraps of conversation are picked up:

RUTH: *(To Ross)* Lena was sick this week . . . strep throat I think. . . . Spent two or three days in bed. . . . Lisa's graduation is coming up and all the affairs to plan. . . . One game of golf with Helen though. . . . Be enough chairs do you think? Don't think Jeffrey will make it, he's got a board meeting in the city this afternoon and might be quite late if it runs on. . . .

This is not a consistent speech, just snatches that float out over the general hubbub as more and more people come in, find places, mill around, and talk.

Among the arrivals are Stanley, a brother of Ben (Lena's father), and also an employee in the family business (his wife Annie and their daughter Elsie are already present); Kenneth, a young man of about 30 who teaches math and does some counseling at the high school; "Doc," who is the town's oldest established general practitioner and the Levin family's physician; Leckner, an eye, ear, nose and throat specialist; and Joshua, who owns and operates a local store. A lawyer or two and a judge join the professional men over cigars and small talk, while their wives chat a bit in another cluster. Susan is Joshua's wife, and they have a daughter, Rita. Elsie, who is Lena's cousin, and Rita help a little with the chairs, but mostly stand attached to their families and finally sit with them. Louise Leckner is a good friend of Ruth's and greets her warmly, helps the hostessing routines along, and finally sits with Leckner—directly facing the network team toward the hallway arch. Their daughter Sara is pretty, mature, and quiet. Susan is a plump, energetic matron who keeps the books in her husband's dry goods store. She has a friendly, self-possessed bluntness that comes from long hours of waiting on customers. Her other daughter Rita slides into the younger set and livens it up, but also seems to crave attention. She looks wan whenever her group pulls

away to help out or she loses the center of attention for some
other reason. After a momentary bit of sulking, she becomes
alert and tries again by finding where the action is and joining
it.

Before she settles down, Dora (Ruth's cousin) shows a
copy of the local weekly paper to Ross. It has a kind of
cryptic gossip column, Cholly Knickerbocker style, and one
paragraph reads: "Guess who are all the folks that are meeting at someone's house to try and solve a local socialite's
problems? We must say it takes a lot of guts to air one's linen
in public, but maybe it will help. Something needs to be done,
and those of us on the outside looking in are pulling for you."

Ross chuckles and passes the paper to Ruth, who blushes
and hurriedly starts to put it behind her back. But Louise
reaches for it, and it circulates for some time, until one of the
older women gets it and, with an outraged look, sits on it.

During this arrival period, there is mounting noise as the
talk and exchange of greetings proceeds. About 100 people
are there by the scheduled time. Except for the absence of
alcohol, this might be a big social party or a group gathering
after the big game. The anxiety everyone feels is masked by
the social roles that are in full swing. It leads to louder and
louder voices and overanimation, while the small talk keeps
things going. When nearly everyone has arrived, Lena makes
her entrance in a baby-doll nightgown—sufficiently opaque
to be decent, but short enough so that without the matching
bloomers, it would be indiscreet indeed. Her hair is short and
straight. Her movements are jerky and graceless, belying the
femininity of her figure. She takes a large pillow and sits on
the floor near her mother's chair, a mixture of small child
and defiant youth. Everyone notices, but tries to avoid giving
any attention or emphasis to the out-of-place costume and
manners. The young people give a low cheer and a couple of
whistles and then return to their own affairs.

During the last five minutes or so, the team has been gathering information and giving it to Ross and Uri, The comments that come out through the buzz include references to the last session, but mostly they are about local current affairs. The group is tense, and the team gets the feeling of two camps having formed. The judge, the two physicians, and several others are on the dining room side; Ruth, Ben, Joshua, and Susan are grouped on the hallway side, facing them.

Many people are standing in both archways and around the edges of the room. They look as if they are in the balcony of a movie theater, or peering at the screen from the lobby —ready to go out for a smoke if the show gets boring or frightening.

Ross stands and claps his hands loudly for attention. He speaks out as the hubbub dies down.

ROSS: There are still a few seats here, and I think we'd better fill them up. *(People leave the dining area reluctantly, as though they might rather delay the start of the meeting.)* There are a few things that I'm going to talk about first, and then I'm going to give you hell. The first thing I want to mention is the Network News—what happened around here this week. Lena called me on the phone a couple of times. I heard from Ruth and Josh when I got here. Lena has been angry at Betty this week, but its been a little better. Maybe it's been because Lena has been sick—she's had some kind of virus apparently, and a throat infection, and has been in bed. And she's here in her nightie tonight —I don't know what its called. She has stayed out of the way of everybody. She says that Ben's OK but that Ruth is no good at all. She hasn't been talking much to Stanley or Lisa. Uh . . . there's been a little more peace in the family. It's kind of an unholy truce though. It's still a difficult situation. Dora showed me the piece in the paper that she thinks refers to these meetings, I guess it does.

Doc told me, and several other people, and he said it several times, "There's a lot of people here who don't know what the hell is going on. . . ." Now this is the third meeting, and we've got just six altogether.

DOC: *(Cutting in)* Including me!

ROSS: Pardon? Including you—well OK. Now we've got *six* times. That's not very many to find out what the hell is going on. What's going on here is that we are training 70, or 60 of you, or however many we've get here, to be psychotherapists and to be intervenors in a family system that keeps reverberating and where everyone is unhappy. You people are supposed to be the friends of at least somebody that's here. If you don't feel friendly to anybody here, and you wonder why the hell you are here, then *I* wonder why the hell you're here? Uh . . . I've been to a lot of these networks, and this is the first one in a real small town, so maybe it's different because everybody knows everybody . . . or maybe really *doesn't* know everybody, because it's a small town . . . but I think there are some factions in here that aren't with this thing at all yet. That's one of those things I've got to talk to you a little more about. There's no way that I can describe things to you. I could give you six sessions of lectures, and maybe you'd know a little more about it. But we're here to do a job . . . and we are here to do that job in a brief period of time.

Brief because look at all the people who are assembled here, and look at the distances that we travel. I've done these things in a year—I've taken a year to do it. We can do it a little more gently that way, but we don't need to if we just remember we're here to do a job. That job is to change the Levin situation, the unlivable situation for each one of them. So that there's a little more peace . . . so that Ben doesn't have to have any more heart attacks . . . so

Lena doesn't have to fall apart with her anxiety all the time
. . . so Lisa can come home from boarding school . . . and
so Ruth can live a little more gracefully than she feels she
does at times. And the way we're going to do it is by
getting you involved as people in this whole process. *(Ross
looks over the group, makes eye contact with a good many,
but avoids recognizing any interruptors.)* You're here, and
you're in on something. I think that most of us are pretty
alienated these days, and you have a chance to come alive
a little bit. Now if you want to fight the chance, you
probably can do that—at least some of you can do that—
and I think there are a lot of people who really wonder
whether they can or will do one damn thing. . . . *(Ross
quickly goes on, preventing interruptions.)* I'm not going to
tell you what to do. Your job is to interfere, to intervene,
to think up solutions—to try solutions—and to push like
hell in this process. We'll have a little bit of that right here
later on, but I'm not going to tell you what that's about
right now.

I think there's a polarity in this group—two sets of
people. I can identify some, and some I can't—but one of
the rules here is to break up secrets, to break up collusions.
To break up the phoniness that goes on in ordinary, everyday relationships. Hopefully, you people will have a tribal
network set up when we leave here such as you've never
had in your lives before. That's hopefully. If you want to,
you can make this your tribe's meeting. If you don't want
it, well, maybe it'll be like it's been. We've got to work on
this polarity in the group. In a minute, I'll give some
instructions about how you do that.

Meanwhile, how about some secrets? . . . Well, there are
a few I've heard. For instance . . . not directly from anyone
. . . but some have gone to other people in the group and
said such things as, "Oh, that guy's a quack, you know he's

not a psychoanalyst. . . . He's just pulling some fakery here. . . ." Uh . . . that's not true! I've worked at this stuff for five years, and I am a psychoanalyst. It just so happens that psychoanalysis couldn't do one thing for this situation. For other situations it's good, but not this one.

Uh . . . there have been a lot of things that I think are the small-town business. A lot of people come around and say to us, "I'm just here because I was invited. . . . I probably wouldn't have come except that I'd probably be looked down on or punished . . . or something like that. . . ." I don't know. . . . I know the Levins fairly well, and I suspect if you really want to skip it, and if that's your only reason for coming . . . I think that you're entitled. Another thing is that I think that there are an awful lot of extremely critical people in this group. Critical meaning *picky* . . . but I don't see them doing very much. So . . . uh . . . we have these two camps: "it's great," or "it's terrible!" I think what I'd like to do is get an open discussion going among you about what I think are the two camps here, about why you're here, and what you should be doing.

JOSHUA: About the Levins? . . .

ROSS: About the Levins, right!

LOUISE: Do you want a group in the center to talk, and who do you think ought to be in it? *(She is over to one side, and makes her way to a chair near Joshua as she talks.)*

ROSS: I, uh . . . I'd like the big group to discuss this.
(There is a pause while people avoid looking at each other and shift a bit. Doc breaks the ice by acting as spokesman.)

DOC: Well, by us coming here as a group . . . and let's say that we do get into a frank discussion. . . . We don't know how that's going to help her, in other words.

ROSS: *(Cutting in and overriding)* You've got to change yourself in order to be able to change somebody else. Unless you're able to get some process of change going in your own lives, you're not going to be able to tell her to get a change going in her life, or Ben's, or Ruth's, or anybody elses'.

DOC: Most people have reservations about exposing something that's intimate to them unless they felt that this is really going to do her some good; and some of these people have expressed this feeling to me, and I agreed with it. I sympathize with it. They are not going to come out here to a group of 50 or 60 people and really expose themselves to something that they think other people are not going to like, unless they know it is really going to do some good. Of course if. . . .

ROSS: *(Cutting in again)* Well, I haven't lost one of these networks yet. They lose 'em in family therapy, and they lose 'em in individual therapy.

DOC: Yeah . . . but. . . .

ROSS: *(Keeping him from continuing)* I haven't lost one of these networks before, and I don't intend to lose on this one. But at the same time, I don't see how I can explain to anybody how this thing works . . . especially if they have already prejudged it. *(Looks about the group)* I'd like the group to discuss this. . . .

(The group is still somewhat frozen, sensing the battle between the two professionals.)

URI: *(Yells, leaning forward in his chair)* Whose side are you on, Doc?

DOC: Which side? *(Puzzled)* You mean for or against?

URI: If you want to put it this way. . . .

DOC: *(Subsiding at this direct challenge)* Well, I'm probably in a neutral camp.

URI: You have to be for or against. Neutral about what? Are you for or against these meetings?

LOUISE: I think it's for or against the method. . . . I think we all want to achieve . . . uh . . . but I don't know what you mean by saying we must change in order to change someone else. . . . We might feel smugly satisfied by what we were doing.

ROSS: That's what I'm saying you do.

SUSAN: But what can we do to change? You tell us. . . .

(Joshua, Doc, and Leckner start talking at once.)

VOICES: We're not going to be. . . . After we leave here. . . . It might be dangerous. I don't know enough about it. The problem is. . . .

(Joshua wins out)

JOSHUA: You mean we're not taking the interest in the Levin family that we should?

URI: You're dead right!

(His emphatic loudness quiets the simmering outburst.)

LOUISE: But did you ever realize that we might think we were bothering people?

LECKNER: *(Overriding the hubbub)* Let me ask you this Dr. . . . You mean that. . . .

URI: Last question!

(His shout silences everybody else.)

LECKNER: *(Continues in spite of heckling)* Are you saying that because we're not changing—and I don't know what you mean by not changing, whether you want me to change my philosophy of life or my attitude towards the Levins—but because we're not changing, we're not contributing to the meeting? My wife says we are smug. . . . Now what do you want me to do—indulge in self-criticism, or criticism of my wife, or of Stanley, or Ruth, or Lena? You're a big man in this field. . . . What is it that you want, that you are critical of?

ROSS: I want your statement of what this group is going to do about the Levin situation.

LECKNER: Well, I'm a neighbor, and I have great affection

for Ben and for Ruth, and for both daughters . . . and I feel very keenly the situation with Lena, and I'd like to help her. But I feel incompetent. I'm not a psychiatrist. . . .

ROSS: *(Looking around for the group of young people)* Janet! Are you around? I said I might call on you. Here you are. *(She looks up, starts to rise, and shakes her hair back out of her face. The group shifts its attention to her—away from the knot of professionals who have been acting as spokesmen—turning a bit in their seats to see who this might be.)*

ROSS: *(To Janet)* What happened in your situation when you weren't going out to work—and how you started to go out to work? Could you tell a little bit of a story about what happened to the network members? Just from one human being who's been through this. . . .

JANET: Well . . . I guess the most obvious thing was that I was very . . . uh . . . moved that all those people were so concerned . . . that they would come and discuss my problems . . . and then offer what they thought were solutions. Of course I rejected almost all of them! But . . . uh . . . I was still impressed by them . . . by their concern. *(She turns a questioning look toward the group, and back toward Ross, as if to say, "Is that what you wanted?")*

ROSS: *(Cutting in and drawing attention back to Janet)* Yes, but I was thinking about Jack. . . . Tell the group what Jack did.

JANET: *(Smiling)* Jack came to the house and practically dragged me off to . . . to work . . . to a job that I had waiting for me.

URI: What time was it?

ROSS: *(Gently ignoring the interruption)* He was going to come and dress you, wasn't he?
(Janet laughs nervously—assenting.)

ROSS: He came and pounded on your bedroom door at 7:30 in the morning.

JANET: Yeah! Well, what impressed me even more . . . there was another lady down the street who actually called her boss and told him that she'd be late that morning. Just to try to help me . . . get dressed and get ready to go out to work.

(Her voice almost breaks as she feels a strong emotion at the fact that somebody actually helped someone like herself. She hurries on to cover it.)

JANET: So . . . I wouldn't say I felt any great change in myself. I was just terribly impressed by . . . what seemed like the kindness of these people. Before that I was always suspicious. . . .

LOUISE: May I ask you how you reacted when these people came?

JANET: I was very suspicious . . . I. . . .

ROSS: You said you were going to call the police. . . .

JANET: *(Indignantly)* But I didn't do it!

ROSS: *(Cajoling, teasing, smiling)* But you said you would!

LOUISE: *(Cutting in)* But would you go along with them . . . the suggestions that they made? . . .

JANET: Eventually I did, but I fought them hard practically the whole way.

LOUISE: Well then we should persist. . . . Is that it?

(Pause and silence—the group is immobilized.)

ROSS: I want the group to discuss this . . . because there are two or three . . . I don't hear. . . .

(A general hubbub breaks out as several people speak at once.)

VOICES: Well maybe. . . . I wonder. . . . But you. . . .

URI: *(Cutting in)* It's hard, there are 40 or 50 people here talking at once. People who want to do something. . . .

LOUISE: *(Clearly—over subsiding noise)* Let me just say that this week we called and wanted her to play golf . . . and she wasn't in . . . and it's true that we didn't call again. . . .

ROSS: Well, this may have been a bad week for that.

LOUISE: Well, we're playing again on Saturday, my daughter and I, and we can ask her about it since she's here. She can speak. . . .

SARA: *(Squirms, but speaks up)* Uh . . . well I phoned her not once but twice. The first time she had a cold, and she wasn't feeling too well. But the second time . . . I wanted to go to the driving range, and I really didn't want to go alone. And I knew Lena likes to play golf, so I called her to come along and shoot a few . . . and she was supposed to call me back. . . . Maybe she did while I was out or something, I don't know. . . . But I wonder, if I call Lena and she says "no," does she really not want me to call? Should I keep on calling? I would very much like to go places and do things with her . . . but. . . .

(Sara trickles off into dead silence as the whole group sits watching intently.)

SARA: *(Finishes lamely)* Uh . . . I don't know whether I should keep calling. . . .

URI: Who's supposed to give you that answer . . . whether you should or shouldn't do it?

SARA: *(Quickly and emphatically)* Lena!

(Long pause—the group is dead silent. Lena looks down, twiddling with the hem of her nightgown, tapping her foot, avoiding everyone's glance.)

URI: You tell yourself . . . your own conscience.

DOC: I think *you* should.

URI: Who do you mean?

DOC: The psychiatrist.

(A hubbub breaks out again.)

VOICES: Experts. . . . But I think. . . . Well if that's. . . . But maybe. . . .

DOC: *(Overriding the noise)* I think you are the experts. . . . And in my opinion, if somebody takes her out and she doesn't like it, you should tell us the best method to pursue. In other words, if somebody comes to take her out and she doesn't want to go, should they continue trying? Should they go back and try it again? In other words. . . .

(Noise drowns him out as everybody tries to talk at once.)

VOICES: Well I think. . . . It looks like. . . . To me it seems. . . . I don't know. . . . I agree, but. . . .

URI: Well, if Dr. Speck told you to insult Lena, would you respect that?

DOC: I sure would!

SARA: Well, I'll tell you what I thought of. If I go every day, she'll . . . until one day, well . . . she will go with me someday.

ROSS: *(Thoughtfully, but getting full attention)* What do you think . . . if she had 75 or 250 phone calls a day . . . that might do? Or 250 people marching through the house and yanking her out of the bathroom, or her bedroom, or something? What do you think that might do?

URI: Not just to Lena, but to Ruth, or to Ben, or Lisa?

LECKNER: May I ask a question of Janet please? You say you had a tendency to reject all these advances of the people who wanted to help you.

(Janet interpolates a "yes" and nods without interrupting. Half of the group, or more, is watching her. A few watch Doc and Leckner—and warily keep an eye on Ross and Uri.)

LECKNER: How long did it take you to change your mind a bit . . . to feel that people were concerned and were trying to help you and weren't going to. . . .

JANET: I . . . uh . . . I don't know . . . I guess maybe I'd say the last three meetings, approximately.

LECKNER: How long after the network started? How long until you became a convert?

JANET: *(Laughs nervously)* About three weeks. . . .

ROSS: *(Deprecatingly)* Well, I wouldn't. . . .

JANET: Yeah, about three weeks until. . . .

(She turns to Ross questioningly. Lena is watching her with narrowed eyes, intently. The group is literally on the edge of their chairs.)

LECKNER: Well, I mean until you realized people were interested?

JANET: Yeah . . . about three weeks. I began to see that. . . . I don't know that I ever really became a convert, uh. . . .

LOUISE: I don't think that we are trying to change Lena. I don't know that we are, necessarily.

ROSS: Yes you are!

(A general hubbub begins, but Louise just raises her voice and goes on over everyone else's efforts to talk.)

LOUISE: I think we are trying to put enough pressure on her . . . and on Ruth and Ben . . . so that they will treat each other in the right way. . . . And the things that are wrong with each other that they can't change, they'll learn to accept.

(One of Ruth's friends, sitting fairly far back, speaks out for the first time.)

WOMAN: You have to remember that we live in a small town, and here we feel pretty close. . . . Did you ever think that maybe we're violating the pride and feelings of a family that doesn't really want to go out with us? Well, maybe then we should leave them alone.

(There are lots of scattered comments for and against this stand, overridden by Ross.)

ROSS: Well, if everybody feels like that, it would give us a clear bill to. . . .

(There is a rise in the level of noise and animation in the room—everybody talking, if not to the total group, to neighbors close by.)

VOICES: Well, I'll take you. . . . Maybe we should. . . . Is it really all right? . . . Can you imagine. . . .

(From the back of the room, a woman's voice prevails over the others, and the rest of the group settles down to listen.)

ANOTHER WOMAN: I'd like to ask another question of Janet. About the network that helped Janet . . . what was it composed of? Who came?

ROSS: Just like this one—neighbors, friends, and relatives. Some people did not know other people in the network. That's usually the case in a city. But in a small town it's different.

SUSAN: Is it better or worse that we know each other?

ROSS: It's worse, I think.

LENA: *(Muttering in the background)* It is worse!

VOICES: Worse. . . . Easier. . . . Who knows everybody?. . .

(Larry, a young lawyer, shakes himself loose from the knot of doctors and other professionals, leans forward, and begins talking. His voice is low, throaty, almost seductive—but not consciously so.)

LARRY: What were the ages of the people in that network?

ROSS: Same as this. . . . I would say that this one is a little younger, there were some older, but pretty much the same.

LARRY: Well, I had a reason for asking. You know, when you talk about some of us going and dragging Lena out. . . . I'm approaching 39, and I've got a law practice and a wife and two kids, and I'm pretty busy. And yet I want to do anything I can, but you know . . . I wouldn't know what to say to her once I got her out of the house. Frankly, in the situation you're talking about, as compared to seeing each other in any kind of a social affair, where we'd normally, any of us, see each other and be involved or what have you. . . . Now, uh . . . people of her own age—her contemporaries—are much more likely to . . . uh . . . have a much better basis for doing this.

ROSS: You've got a lot more to offer though than what you're. . . .

LARRY: But I'm not so sure that I might say something that isn't horribly wrong, and I don't want to do that. . . . *(There is a low background hum of comments among the group.)*

VOICES: She's a girl, isn't she?. . . It's the generation gap. . . . I feel uncomfortable. . . .

LARRY: *(Continues)* By "something horribly wrong," I don't mean "insulting," I mean it's not my business. . . . *(The hubbub is building in the background.)*

ROSS: *(Clearly, so the whole group can hear)* You've got to take a chance.

LARRY: *(Continues doggedly)* We're talking about two professions . . . and if it were my family, for example, this is *my* responsibility. When. . . .

URI: *(Loudly, pointedly—moving abruptly to confront Larry across the fireplace)* If you feel that way, why are you here? *(The rest of the group subsides to listen.)*

LARRY: I'm here because I was told . . . of this, uh, thing, this network, which I had never heard of before . . . and nothing about how it worked. I was asked to come and take part and do what I could.

URI: *(Cutting in quickly, almost cutting him off)* How do you perceive your role here? Up to tonight?

LARRY: Why . . . uh . . . I don't know . . . uh, this is the. . . .

URI: I'll tell you how I perceive it. *(Drowning out Larry's*

efforts to continue) I perceive your role as "curious specta-
tor."

*(Murmurs from the group—Larry flushes angrily, shrugs,
and then verbalizes his anger, his voice having lost its silki-
ness.)*

LARRY: You have a right to say anything, anything you
please! I wonder what it is you expect? I was here last week
for the first time. . . .

URI: *(Taking charge of the total group)* I'd like to change. I
think that what you are saying is right. I think that you
are not the only one.

*(Continues in machine-gun-like staccato speech, looking
around the room)* Ninety-nine percent of the people here
are spectators!

*(Sheer bedlam breaks out as many people try to talk at the
tops of their voices. The gloves are off now, and lots of people
want a piece of the action. The room is charged with emotion.)*

VOICES: We are not! Ruth, you know we are your friends.
. . . Of course, my dear. . . . Looky here, that's not the
way to talk. . . . Well, I never heard. . . . Can I say
something? . . .

*(Leckner rises and stands by the fireplace across from Uri,
as Larry takes his chair. He begins to speak. His voice is
quiet but authoritative, and the hubbub subsides.)*

LECKNER: Let me say something to Uri. You're an aggres-
sive, articulate person and . . . now I'm not trying to
psychoanalyze you. . . .

ROSS: Oh yes, you are!

LECKNER: *(Shrugs this off and continues addressing Uri directly)* You're trying to stimulate discussion, but without
any guidelines. Meanwhile . . . now I'm cooperative . . .
I'm not here as a curiosity seeker. I want to help. I came

home the other day from the office and I took Lena out
to play golf. I insisted that she do it.

ROSS: *(In background)* Great!

LECKNER: And she was sick when she went out, and I didn't
know it. She went home with a fever . . . ever since then.
So I don't think that was much help.

(There are murmurs of assent from many in the group.)

LECKNER: Now you'll have to tell me . . . What else do you
want me to do? Do you want me to criticize Lena? Or my
wife?

LOUISE: *(Speaks up teasingly)* You'd better not!

(Much laughter)

URI: The only thing we can say to you is you have to do
what your feeling tells you to do . . . what you feel you can
do.

LECKNER: Well, I . . . uh. . . . *(Covers his confusion by turning
to look for a seat)*

URI: Oh, you're leaving! Fine!

LECKNER: Well, frankly, I'm in a dilemma. . . .

WOMAN: *(In background)* So am I.

*(Joshua, a short, barrel-chested man in a sport shirt and
crepe-soled shoes, rises to his feet. He bounces as he talks.)*

JOSHUA: Action speaks louder than words. Isn't that right?
You're not interested in words now. You want us to do
something.

*(A general hubbub breaks out and then subsides—as atten-
tion shifts to Annie, Ruth's sister-in-law.)*

ANNIE: Many of us here have really put forth an effort
. . . on your project. We've done everything we possibly
could, we've called and tried in every direction.

ANOTHER WOMAN: Sometimes you have the feeling you may
be prying where you're not wanted, you know.

LOUISE: *(The peacemaker)* When anybody said they thought

it was disgraceful, they didn't mean that we thought the meeting was disgraceful, but that it was embarrassing for people to have to hear. . . .

ROSS: *(Quietly)* It is embarrassing.

RUTH: *(Speaking out for the first time)* I'm really embarrassed by the whole thing. It's pretty lousy to wash out your dirty laundry in front of everybody. *(Takes a deep breath)* However, there are a lot of people here who have tried to get Lena out . . . and she pretty much makes them nervous, so they say, "Oh, the heck with it!" There are some here who wonder, "What am I calling for? She ought to be going out with kids her own age." And they mean well. But even I couldn't say what is the right thing. I don't know either. I've tried my damnedest to get Lena out.

LENA: *(Speaks for the first time)* What about this week? . . .

URI: *(Pouncing on the opportunity)* Come on Lena. Come on over here.

(Lena moves slowly, but flouncily, to a spot near the center of the fireplace—not taking either side.)

DOC: Well, there are a lot of people here who wonder if Lena has been out when she shouldn't have been out. Now when I saw her in the office, I said, "How are you doing?" She said, "I went out and played golf." I said, "How'd you do?" I think that approach is very good, because she said, "I'd of beat hell out of you!" So she does accept this approach from us.

(At this capitulation from the opposition camp, the talk gets very animated and builds in loudness. This hubbub is different from the social chitchat of the premeeting gathering —and free of the apologetic and angry comments of before. People are involved in talking about what has been going on and what they now see as ways of acting and approaching the situation. They are also expressing their feelings openly about the rejections and rebuffs.)

WOMAN: Well, when that happened, I said to myself. . . .

MAN: *(Possibly Leckner speaking to Larry)* When she told me on the phone at the last minute that she wasn't coming, I told her she was rude and inconsiderate, and I wasn't going to take it. . . .

ANOTHER MAN: I'd like to give them hell, but of course I can't do it because I'd lose their trade. . . .

ANOTHER MAN: That girl needs a paddling right on the ass, but boy you just can't do that and get away with it. . . .

JOSHUA: *(Moves over and confronts Lena)* The basic fact is that none of us can go around this world doing what we goddamn feel like. . . .

LENA: *(Sarcastically)* I tried to.

JOSHUA: You got away with a hell of a lot more than you should.

LENA: Right you are!

JOSHUA: Yes, because somebody is afraid they might hurt your feelings.

LENA: Oh, really? Sour grapes!

ANOTHER MAN: How long do you think this has been going on?

LENA: A few years?

MAN: It's always been that way . . . believe me.

LENA: Always?

(While these exchanges have been going on, the team members have been having conferences—around the edges. The noise of the rest of the talk has been covering their activities, and no one is missing them. The exchanges between people float out clearly over the general talk. Ross comes back to the central spot by the fireplace and stands there a few seconds, focusing attention on himself.)

ROSS: I've just heard that there are a lot of hiding-behind-the-couch psychoanalysts around, and that they are afraid of stirring up any trouble. That they are walking on eggshells. That they want to keep things just kind of nice and polite. But if we do that, it leaves things status quo—then we won't get the network effects that Lena, and her mother, and everybody else want.

LENA: I think a lot of the people here are superficial and they are fakes. They just came to see the circus.

URI: Aw, Lena. . . . Come on now, everybody?

(There is an outbreak of protest over which Uri keeps asking Lena to commit herself, while she indignantly and angrily spits venom on the group.)

URI: *(Finally gains control)* Come on now . . . let me help you. Everybody you see here? Or just some of them? . . .

LENA: Everybody!

URI: Let's see the people you can trust and who care for you. Right now! Who cares for you?

LENA: Elsie, where's Elsie?

(Elsie is a cousin who hasn't spoken yet.)

RUTH: You fight with Elsie. You just name her because you haven't seen her for a while. . . .

LENA: *(To Ruth—her mother)* You just wanted me to call on you. . . . You've been just a pearl this week.

URI: Who else in the group?

LENA: Sara.

URI: Who else in this group? There are 70 people here. Who else cares for you?

LENA: Uncle Stanley.

ANNIE: *(Speaks up)* I think we're being a little hard on Lena. She does some nice things, too, that I know about.

URI: OK, you tell us about them.

ANNIE: Well she plays golf better than I do. *(Laughs self-consciously)* I used to play with her when she was learning, and now she's so good I can't call her to play with me. . . .

ROSS: *(Firmly but quietly)* Yes you can.

ANNIE: And then when my son was coming home from his mother-in-law's funeral that nobody else could go to, Lena was the one who met him at the airport. So I can say she has never been ugly to me. . . .

ELSIE: *(Loud, strident, involved)* Can I put my two cents in? Everybody is being too damned careful of what they say to Lena. If I get mad, I tell her. If she gets mad at me, that means she'll yell at me . . . so what?

(Uri breaks in, outshouting Elsie and cutting off more of her speech along the same lines. Throughout this sequence he is like a terrier with a cat, never letting up—not hurting Lena, but allowing no escape from his bark or his pounce.)

URI: I want to ask a question. . . . I want to know this . . . you tell me, or if that's too hard to tell me, tell the group . . . all these people here . . . why are they so hypocritical? That's what you call them anyway. Why are they?

LENA: *(Strident, excited, but thoughtful)* Why are they?

URI: Yes.

LENA: Why are these people fakes? . . . Well, I'm sitting here, and I see these deep, deep, deep emotions, and they just can't . . . and I don't think they will. And maybe . . . well, I've heard . . . "Well, if it's all up to me. . . ." and "I just don't know how we can do it." And uh. . . .

URI: Why is that? Do you think they can't . . . if they want to?

LENA: They say they can't.

URI: Are you sure they *can?*

LENA: Well, gee if this ever happened to them, I could do it.

URI: All these people here . . . they *can* help you? If they want to?

LENA: Yes, if they want to.

URI: *(Keeping the pace going)* How can they help you?

LENA: *(Startled)* How can they?

URI: Yes, tell us how.

LENA: *(Deflated)* Gosh, I don't know. I haven't thought about it.

URI: *(A little more gently, but still firm)* Well think about it.

LENA: *(On the edge of sullenness—still thinking)* Yeah, well . . . I will!

(She turns away a little, frowning in concentration. Larry speaks up, more naturally this time. He is no longer Jimmy Stewart in "Mr. Smith Goes to Washington," but seems genuinely to be seeking information.)

LARRY: Lena, I know you're pretty much into golf. What other things do you like to do or not do . . . or like to do, maybe, that would work out better?

RUTH: *(Prompts a little with a quiet word)* Scrabble. . . .

LENA: *(Quiet, shy, smiles, looks down and fingers hem of the babydoll gown)* Well, I like to play scrabble. . . .

LARRY: *(Leaning forward and talking directly to Lena— preventing Ruth and Annie from prompting her)* You're a game person? . . . You like games?

LENA: *(Brightening up)* Yes.

(Several people in the group try to talk at the same time.)

LARRY: *(Waving them off)* Wait a minute. . . .

(The hubbub continues.)

JOSHUA: *(Finally gains the floor)* Hey, wait a minute. You know where my son is now?

LENA: *(Turns, startled, but still in low key)* No. . . .

JOSHUA: He's playing Little League. Guess where I turn out to be. . . . Why are Dora and I here? Because we don't like you? Why did we drive you home the other night when you'd taken a sleeping pill and you were afraid you'd fall asleep? Because we don't like you?

LENA: *(Indignantly)* I didn't say you don't like me!

JOSHUA: *(Pushing for his point)* We are not trying to help *you*? Because the man said maybe if we could come here that we could help you? I don't understand! You're looking at the people here that you don't like! Why are we here?

LENA: You tell me why you're here! You tell me you are here because you were asked to come here!

SUSAN: *(Quietly)* No, because. . . .

(Everyone starts talking at once, all loudly protesting that they didn't just come because they were asked.)

LARRY: Now wait a minute. *I* said that! No. . . . I wouldn't be here if I weren't asked. Obviously . . . I mean nobody would. Secondly, I've got an office full of work I should be doing, and I am here because I'd like to help. I didn't, uh . . . when I said I came because I was asked to come . . . I didn't mean, well I'm going to come and then I'm going to sit. But you've got to give me some answers, too! For example—the last time I was in contact with you was at the cquntry club party. I tried to talk with you . . . we sat at the same table.

LENA: *(Cutting in)* We did?

LARRY: Well, you wouldn't talk to me! And I finally gave up.

LENA: How were you at the table? There was me, and my sister, and Dad, and. . . .

RUTH & BEN: *(Muttering in the background)* Your party was at a different table. Come on man, you didn't go with us. . . .

LARRY: *(Clarifying and outtalking the confusion)* At one point, my wife was dancing with someone else, and I didn't feel like dancing, and you were all alone at the table . . . so I sat down. I sat down one chair over from you, and then I moved into the empty chair next to you, and tried to talk to you. . . . Maybe you don't like to talk.

(Lena keeps protesting that this isn't the same as being with her all evening.)

LARRY: *(Refuses to allow interruptions—continues doggedly)* That's not the point. Maybe you don't like small talk. But

you've got to tell me at least what you like to do. You
mentioned games. . . . Now I'm not a game person.
(Laughter) I'm serious. I hate to play games. But my wife
and daughter, though, they adore it. You can come over
and play with them all day and all night. That would be
terrific! But if you want me to help, you've got to tell me
—and the others—what kind of things you like to do.

RUTH: *(To Larry)* Aren't you being a little harsh?

(Lena glares at her and turns her back.)

LARRY: No, the point I'm making, Lena . . . if you want to
get out of the house or anything, you've got to *want* to.
What do you want? Then maybe we can help. What are
you interested in? What do you like? Do you follow me?

LENA: *(Thoughtful, almost dreamy)* I . . . I'd like a job . . .
I'd like to, uh . . . get back to school . . . and get some
education. . . .

*(Larry's deep, seductive voice is back now that there is no
competing noise and he is getting direct responses from
Lena.)*

LARRY: Well, Lena, maybe that's what we need to help with.
But you dropped out of school over the same things that
are bothering you now. We've got to do something else
first. What are the everyday things that we need to help
with or that you want?

LENA: *(Angry, indignant, and spiteful)* You *are* just a fake!
I knew you wouldn't listen if I did say anything. You're
just being a hypocrite like the rest of them!

*(This provokes a general outburst of remarks—both retal-
iating and conciliatory.)*

LARRY: *(Prevailing over the confusion—continuing matter-of-
factly)* I just asked you a question. You have no right to
talk to me that way. Now we heard during the first part
of the evening that we were all being passive and resistant
—so I'll try to be active and positive . . . And I'm sure

whatever I have to say, your feelings will be constant, and it won't make any difference . . . but I'm going to go ahead. . . .

LENA: Why all the commotion then?

LARRY: Because I think that's what the doctors want us to do. . . . Lena, you're lazy, you're indifferent, you're inconsiderate. You worked for me in the office. You did typing. You did a good job. I was happy to have you, and I wanted to keep you on. And I said to you, "Lena, I want you to learn to use the dictaphone."

LENA: *(Angrily and sarcastically)* And just because I didn't know how to use the dictaphone, all the girls turned against me, and whatever else I did wasn't any good.

LARRY: No, you told the girl in my office you didn't want to learn because you'd have to work.

LENA: Aw . . . she can go to hell.

LARRY: You told Katy that.

LENA: I did not.

(She starts shouting and name-calling over another general outbreak of shocked exclamations.)

LARRY: Before any help works, Lena, you're going to have to change.

LENA: Why should I have to change? You tell me that? A lot of people around here ought to change!

URI: *(Strongly enough to get Lena's attention and silence Larry)* Who are you going to change, Lena?

LENA: My parents.

URI: Who?

LENA: My parents, my sister. . . .

URI: Wait a minute. One at a time now. Your mother. . . .

(During this exchange, they are shouting each other down, facing each other.)

LENA: Yeah!

URI: What should she change to? How is she going to change?

LENA: *(Indignantly)* I don't know how she's going to change. . . .

URI: What should she change to?

LENA: *(A little more quietly—beginning to think)* She should make an effort to understand. . . .

DOC & BEN: *(Cutting in to defend Ruth)* Just a minute, Lena. Now, you know your mother tries.

LENA: *(Shouting again)* I'm trying to talk now. Let me finish!

DOC: Just one question. . . .

URI: *(Glares him down)* Let Lena finish. The rules are one person talks at a time around here. Lena, go on.

LENA: *(Slowly and thoughtfully)* She should make an effort to understand this thing . . . and . . . to change some of her thoughts. . . . So it's not just "Lena, Lena, Lena."

URI: Uh huh . . .

LENA: *(Suddenly speeding up her rate of speech—as if somebody might cut her off before it is all out)* And so should my father and my sister. I hear Lisa saying all the time, "I don't want to get involved . . . I don't want to get involved." Why shouldn't she? She lives here!

URI: Uh huh. How should Lisa change?

LENA: *(Slowly again)* Well, she's such a distant person. She doesn't wanna get involved. . . . *(Faster—her voice rising)* I mean she's very selfish! Well, outside she's such a nice sweet little girl, but on the inside she's like a big rock and always wants to stop and watch this thing. . . . And she's cold and she's selfish and uh. . . . *(Trails off)* And that's what I think of her.

URI: How about your Daddy?

LENA: Huh?

URI: Your Daddy. How about him?

LENA: He's a little better. I think it's hard to make a comparison. But . . . uh . . . I still think that he has to change to a degree that when I tell him something which he disagrees with . . . with me . . . that he stops saying: *(Imitates his sarcastic and placating tone)* "That's right Lena. You're right and the world's wrong!" You know, that's his stock answer today, if he, uh . . . disagrees with something I have to say.

URI: Now I have one last question, and then we can have group discussion. How about you? How do you have to change?

LENA: *(Scoffing)* Oh, a lot a ways. I could write a book about me. . . .

URI: Well tell us now, what do you have to change?

LENA: *(Directly to Uri—almost as if she has forgotten the silent audience in the room)* I have to change plenty!

URI: Huh, I didn't get that.

DOC: *(Butting in)* She says she has to change plenty, but she didn't *try.*

URI: *(Putting his shoulder between them)* Tell us more specifically, Lena. . . . Like you did about your sister.

LENA: Well, I've got to see myself . . . uh . . . in order to help myself. . . .

URI: Tell us about yourself.

LENA: It's hard. . . . Uh . . . I think I may have to change and understand other people . . . be kind of aware of other people . . . and try not to think so much of the time about myself . . . as I do . . . or at least as I'm accused of. . . . And uh. . . .

URI: And that's it?

LENA: No, there's more.

(As she pauses thoughtfully, you can hear a pin drop. Everyone is frozen, intent, not drawing on their cigarettes or pipes, or shifting in their chairs—as if they were afraid that a movement would break the spell.)

LENA: I, uh . . . I guess I'll have to think about it. I just can't . . . uh . . . seem to talk about it right now. . . .

URI: Well, maybe then this is a good place for a group discussion.

(There is silence for half a minute or more. Then Jacob, who hasn't spoken before, leans forward and speaks softly.)

JACOB: Let me ask Lena. Lena, if you really want to change. . . .

LENA: Certainly I want to change.

JACOB: When I had my breakdown, and then came out of it, I had to realize it was up to me. Nobody was going to do it for me. It was up to me.

(The group is still frozen, not even a gasp, as they realize that this is the first time Jacob has referred to his own hospitalization publicly. It is as though they were eavesdropping on a private dialogue.)

LENA: I realize some of that. A lot of it I suppose has to come from within. But why do they always put it all on me? You're really in a bind then, if they don't help too, and if you're living with your family at the time. They can't change either—so it's always Lena this and Lena that. Well, I think it's my parents, too. I don't think it's all me.

JACOB: Well, yes, it's true the whole environment counts. But somehow it goes together—you have to see the light before the changes do any good.

RUTH: I think I begin to see that Lena wants to change . . . and I think maybe I have to change myself. . . . For as long as I can remember, I've been trying to change things, and I haven't changed much yet, but. . . .

LECKNER: Lena, suppose you could get out of here. Suppose you were living someplace else, in your own apartment somewhere . . . and you had to get to work, because if you weren't getting your paycheck this week, you couldn't make the payment on your car or something . . . and you

had to work to take care of these certain obligations you
had. . . . You could not afford the luxury of staying in bed
because maybe you didn't feel good . . . and. . . .

LENA: I would like to state that I was in bed this past week
because of my virus, not because of my so-called luxury.

JOSHUA: There have been times when you stayed in bed
because you just weren't feeling like going to work! Am I
right or wrong?

LENA: Well, there were plenty of times when I pushed myself
to get up.

JOSHUA: Well, sometimes with a virus you have to push
yourself, too. Suppose you had to—you just had to?

LOUISE: *(Breaks in)* Suppose there was someplace you had
to be every morning, and no one else could do it for you
—people were depending on you?

*(The group erupts loudly with similar questions, and Lena
angrily twists and turns, shouting them down in her own
defense. The spell is broken, and the anger of the group
reasserts itself—trying to force Lena to change. Everybody
is talking at once again, letting her feel the pressure—and
the noise level rises to a crescendo. Almost in midstream, the
attack turns from Lena to her parents.)*

LENA: But I'm not the only one around here.

VOICES: I don't know Ruth, why don't you just get her
up? . . . Ben, you aren't that helpless. If Lena was my kid,
I . . . well . . . I think if it was me. . . .

*(This outbreak of affect still falls short of mobilization. The
group is still assessing blame—attempting to assign responsibility to others. As the hubbub escalates, the team with-
draws briefly to the archway of the hall.)*

ROSS: I'm restless—we've almost broken through a couple of
times, but this resistance to involvement is terrific.

SOCIAL WORKER: *(To Ross and Uri)* The people in back
aren't fighting you two any more, but they still haven't

committed themselves to any action. They seem like a
bunch of confused parents who don't know what to do
except punish and scold. There's a lot of depression here,
and I think the anger comes out as a defense against it.

URI: It's time to implode the system. We've got to change our
tactics.

ROSS: I checked with Ben's doctor, and he says his heart
could stand some strain for one evening—especially if it
wasn't a combination of emotions and activity. Let's get
the focus off Lena and onto them . . . the parents.

URI: I've got an idea. You get back there and be ready to help
control the traffic—you and the others. I want them to all
come up, one at a time, and talk—you'll see. *(Strides
purposefully back to the center by the fireplace and claps
his hands for attention)* We're going to try something else
now. All of you move back and clear a space here. . . .
(Indicates a central area) May I have that chair please—
and that one. Thank you. *(Puts two straight chairs side by
side in the center, with space all around)* Now, Ruth, I
want you and Ben to sit here, side by side. That's it. Do
you ever hold hands? *(Embarrassed laughter)* I think you
should now. Just hold on to each other and close your
eyes. The way things are going, you feel like the only two
people in the world. . . . You wonder what all these other
people are really thinking and feeling. No—don't say anything. There are just the two of you for a moment. Now,
I have a task for the rest of you. . . . Line up over there
and come up one at a time to these two people. I want you
to touch them . . . and I want you to tell them what you
are really thinking and feeling—how you truly feel about
them.
*(The group looks around, restless but silent. Ruth and Ben
are now sitting alone in the center. A few people stand
awkwardly to the sides where they have been moved out of*

the way. Lena is near Uri and Ross, on the edge of things.)

URI: That's right, stand up over here. And each of you, including Lena, come on up one at a time and tell them your right feelings—each of them—what you think of them . . . as a parent.

ROSS: As a person, too, I think.

URI: Yes . . . OK . . . but your right feelings.

DOC: The good and the bad?

URI: No more questions—just do it. Who is ready to start? I want each and every one of you to come up in this group . . . including Lena.

(There is a little background muttering, ever since Doc's question.)

LOUISE: *(To Uri)* You mean what we think will help them?

ROSS: Be friendly. I don't know what will help them—neither do you . . . but be friendly and honest.

MAN: How can we be friendly if we don't know 'em? I went to a game with him once, and I knew he enjoyed it and looked forward to it. And we made movies of it. But when it comes to your daughter, I don't know them. I don't know how you brought them up. That's your business. I think at times we have discussed it, but . . . now we are getting blamed for it. But these are the things . . . the way you are acting makes me feel. . . . I don't know why you did what you did. . . . Every time you've done anything for us, you've never asked anything in return . . . never any. I've got an extra ticket to the game, come on! Or . . . I don't know why you asked us here when we can't seem to do anything . . . as people.

(The man gives way to his wife, who stands in front of the couple.)

WOMAN: You're the best neighbors I've ever had, Ruth. You're lots of fun. Ben, you're kind, generous, and . . . I think you're not consistent enough in your treatment

to your children. . . . On the one hand, you treat them
as two . . . uh, juveniles . . . and on the other hand,
you expect them to be adults . . . and there you are. . . .
*(She reaches out and grasps their clasped hands, then
retires blushing.)*

URI: *(Quietly)* Thank you. *(Guides the couple away and turns
back)* Next!

BEN: Doc. . . . How about this? Do we get a rebuttal, or what?

URI: You have to listen. . . . No rebuttal now, maybe
later. . . .
*(Meanwhile, Larry, the lawyer, has come into position. He
puts his hands on Ben and Ruth's.)*

LARRY: I can't say too much. I feel that's its been a privilege
to have been a friend of Ben, here—and Ruth, too, and
their children. I have so much love and compassion for all
of you that this hurts me deeply . . . what I see now.
. . . The only thing I can say . . . just . . . just that. . . .
*(Another couple is by the tape recorder now, and their voices
come out strongly as they talk to one another, waiting their
turn.)*

MAN: This feels like an Irish wake.

WOMAN: Yes, it does.
(Another man stands briefly in front of Ben and Ruth.)

ANOTHER MAN: I think it's a privilege to tell you how I feel.
(He touches them and moves on.)

JOSHUA: *(Doesn't sound like himself)* Ruth and Ben, I've
known you for about 14 years, and now you've been very
kind and invited us to your home. Lena's been in the store
a number of times. . . . Perhaps if she had a purpose and
responsibility, maybe she wouldn't be having so many
problems.

BEN: Thank you.

URI: *(Cutting off interaction)* Next.

(Stanley, Ben's brother, clears his throat loudly, then clears it again. He can't seem to get started.)

URI: If you feel like taking their hand, or touching instead of talking, by all means. . . .

(Stanley starts to reach out, but decides to talk instead. The throat clearing gone, his voice is high.)

STANLEY: I guess I've known you a long while, Ben . . . you've always been good to work for. . . . Ruth, you've had a tough time recently. . . . *(Stronger)* You've come through it a hundred percent! And I think if we can cooperate a little bit more, everything will be . . . uh, solved.

(He drops back with a sort of pat at the couple—moving over for the next person.)

MAN: Well, Ben, I don't feel that I know you as well as some of the other adults. But . . . well, let me just give my feelings as parents and people. Well, as parents I don't know of anything I can say . . . that would be critical . . . or, on the other hand, beneficial. . . . As people, well you've always been very nice to me . . . personally . . . and what I feel now is complete, uh, despair on your part.

URI: *(Quietly)* Thank you.

(There is always a slight pause between speakers, as Uri regulates the traffic. A woman comes up, takes a deep breath, and plunges in—talking quickly.)

WOMAN: I've known Ruth much longer than I've known Ben. We've been friends for many years and done things together. Ben has been a very good golfer and very fair . . . and I like you. *(Moves off abruptly)*

URI: Excellent.

(Another woman, a slightly older relative, stands in front of them. Tears begin pouring down her face.)

WOMAN: Ben, you're my nephew. . . . And I love Ruth . . . you are not a cold person, and I love that in you. . . . *(Her voice breaks)* There just aren't many other people in this world that mean as much to me . . . I just love you so much.

(Some of the others help her away with a handkerchief and a cold drink, and the next woman steps in quickly. Ruth is letting tears fall, now, and Ben will in a few minutes.)

WOMAN: I can't think of anything to say—except that this hurts, and I just want to tell you, "hello."

MAN: I guess what she says goes for myself. . . .

(He puts his hand on Ben's arm and moves off as tears begin.)

LECKNER: *(Sounds very far away)* I feel very . . . very . . . small here . . . and helpless. . . .

(He clasps each of their free hands in one of his and turns away.)

MAN: You've both helped me—you both know that. . . . If there's a conflict, I guess you just have to resolve it. . . . You're strong people . . . but I don't know. . . .

(He drops a pat on their hands and turns away snuffling. By now the crying is contagious, affecting nearly the entire group. The room is absolutely silent, except for the movement of people between speakers—and even this is now scarcely audible. Each one comes forward to stand, touch, and speak with his head down. They tend to reach out quickly, as though the need to replace or relieve the previous person was as great as the need to offer comfort to Ruth and Ben.)

WOMAN: Well now, Ben and Ruth, I feel so sorry about all this. . . . I'd do anything if. . . . When she used to come into our home, she's so very congenial, and she's met with us and socialized. . . . And then when she came home from school, its been so different. It's just . . . I don't know. . . .

ANOTHER WOMAN: I just feel terrible. . . .

(She stands there a moment and then Uri takes her elbow

—passing her on to the group that has already spoken. Uri's voice is choked too, and his manner is almost like that of an usher at a funeral parlor, but more real. He turns to the waiting line.)

URI: How about you, Ma'am?

WOMAN: I can say that next to my husband, I love Ben as dearly as I do my brother. I've been as close as . . . closer than a sister to Ruth for the past 25 years. There isn't anybody any closer to me . . . than these two people and their children. . . . And I would do anything to help them, and I think they know it! And I have extended myself, but I still will do anything to help you both.

DOC: I don't have to say anything—about affection for Ruth and Ben. They know it. You're faced with a dilemma. I've, ah . . . as you told me, Ben, "Don't give me solutions." I'm not a psychiatrist. You've got a big problem . . . and I'd like to help all I can. I just hope as a human being you come out all right, and I hope the psychiatrists know what they are doing!

DOC'S WIFE: Well, I agree with my husband's statement, and I know that most of us have our problems here . . . and don't blame yourselves for anything. Don't blame Lena. Let's just come on and. . . . Oh, I don't know what to say. It's a dreadful feeling.

(Doc takes his wife away gently, his arm around her, his professional armor melted.)

URI: And you?

WOMAN: *(Shakily)* Well . . . Ruthy, she's my cousin. . . . And Ben, I've known you for a long time. I feel just like I did when I lost my mother—I don't know if you can understand this at all . . . but somewhere we can help you.

URI: Thank you . . . and now you.

YOUNGER WOMAN: There are a lot of very wet eyes in this

room right now. But I see a lot of lack of emotion in Lena, even when we're sitting right here. I don't know what to make of it.

URI: Carry on.

MAN: *(Looks down—talking only to Ben and Ruth)* You came to my wedding, and you've been very good to work for. . . . And I hope you know how much I love you both . . . how much I want to help. . . .

WOMAN: There hasn't been a time when you weren't somebody important in our lives. . . . But I've always looked to you, and now I guess you need help.

URI: Lena?

(She steps in front of her parents—talking quickly, but not defiantly. There is tension in her voice, making it hard to understand; but it doesn't show in her posture, which seems calm, detached, almost distant.)

LENA: I just feel cold, selfish, tired . . . and I wish we could get this straightened out. . . . I get completely tired of . . . oh . . . people, I do love you but . . . also having no real faith . . . I wish to hell we could get it straightened out. I wish we could try this more—and not be cold and mean . . . and superficial to our neighbors. . . .

URI: Next.

MAN: I, uh . . . think Ben and Ruth kind of like . . . you're, uh . . . my cousins. Ben's got a heart of gold, and Ruth can be, uh . . . hardheaded at times. But, uh . . . how she can get up and say the things she did, while her daughter kicks her in the ass, is beyond me.

JANET: I don't think that's fair. I don't think we should criticize Lena under those circumstances. She was supposed to come up and say something to Ruth and Ben— and not to figure out how they would feel, or what they would say . . . and why Lisa can be like us, and Lena can't.

. . . And I can't just stand there and let it go by. . . .

ROSS: Let's not get distracted now and get in a fight. It's your turn to talk to Ruth and Ben.

JANET: *(Continues)* I guess so . . . but I don't know what to say, because I've been listening to everybody. . . . *(Turns to face the couple—touching first one and then the other impulsively as she speaks)* We care! We're here! *(Draws back)* Yes, we are here. *(Turns to Ross and Uri)* You asked us to come up and tell what we thought as parents, right?

ROSS: *(Almost whispers)* Of them as parents.

JANET: *(Continues)* "Of them as parents," is what I meant to say. And people come up to say you're wonderful people . . . you're great friends . . . and I feel like an absolute stinker to say the things that I've been thinking. But I don't know what else to say because. . . .

RUTH: Say them!

JANET: OK. Well, it seems to me that there's been a great emphasis on going places, doing things—let's go here, and let's do that. Maybe I'm projecting from myself. I need somebody to talk to. And I don't know much about your family—how it works and what the situation is. I think that talk and understanding means a lot . . . and that . . . uh, Lena criticizes you . . . and that you say she has problems . . . and I think it needs give and take on both sides. . . . And sometimes I get real confused, because sometimes it was said that Lena couldn't make the bed because she was sick and . . . and then at other times it was forgotten that, uh . . . you know, that Lena was sick. . . . And I know it's difficult, but I think Lena has to be given extra consideration.

URI: *(Cutting in)* Thank you.

WOMAN: I feel sorry for you as I would any parents . . . that went through what I did with my sister.

URI: Thank you.

(A man comes next and puts one hand on each of the parents' shoulders. His words, and his feeling, and the breaks in his voice, and his touching are all part of his communication.)

MAN: I keep feeling I want to grab my wife and go home and sit down with my own kids and make them understand us —and vice versa.

(A woman comes up and mumbles something—looking down and twisting her handkerchief.)

URI: *(Quietly)* Can't you hold their hands?

WOMAN: *(Jumps as though startled out of a dream)* Oh . . . sure I can. *(Reaches out)* I feel sorry for you—and I hope it gets straightened out as soon as possible.

(Several people in turn step up—touching and murmuring softly to Ben and Ruth. They are not talking to the larger group, but directly to the couple—in intimate, almost non-verbal contact. The fourth or fifth man speaks loudly enough to be heard. He is one of the doctors in the group, a pediatrician.)

MAN: I guess you know that you are fun to be with . . . are kind and generous and always considerate . . . and always have been. As parents, well, I've observed them. I've lived in this town for over 30 years. They are no different—no better and no worse—than the average parent that I run into. If you're too kind, people say you're to easy. . . . If you're too harsh, they would have said you were impossible, but it would have no meaning to it. All I can say is that there is nothing on your part that calls for a psychiatrist. You've acted exactly like any other parent. . . . And so far as Lena is concerned, she has a problem, but we're going to beat it.

WOMAN: I welcome the opportunity to be here . . . and to be part of this, because I hardly ever get to talk to you. . . . And it doesn't seem to me you've been getting much help here . . . but maybe you'll find things different now.

URI: Next—anybody else here?

MAN: *(One of the younger men steps up and has Ben feel his shoes.)* I used to come into this house, and I walked barefooted—so I think I know you very well. And I can say this . . . I think you're very nice people . . . as good friends and neighbors as I could want. . . . And maybe you're the same as many people that have money and not too much to worry about . . . and maybe you've lost contact with one another—as parents.

(Lena's grandfather is next.)

GRANDFATHER: I don't believe that. It's just something that has happened. . . . It could happen to poor, poor people. It could happen to rich, rich people . . . and I sure as heck hope it gets resolved.

URI: Thank you.

MAN: Well Ben and Ruth—as parents, uh . . . you're just like I am. You're confused and do things like I do . . . and you're overjoyed and happy on occasion, and you're very sad on other occasions as we are . . . as we are. I think it's an unfortunate situation. . . . I think that this happened because possibly your little chick didn't quite go out of the nest when she should have . . . when she had a chance . . . but it's not as hopeless as bucking city hall.

WOMAN: You know my heart is with you, Ruth. I'm turning 40, and so is my sister-in-law . . . and we have been to doctors too. . . . *(Pecks Ruth on the cheek and steps back.)*

At this point, it is probably a good idea to interrupt the transcript and point out that it has taken a good 45 minutes for these first couple of dozen speakers—and there are about 100 people in the room. At least another hour is spent in exactly this same way—network members coming up one at a time, touching, speaking, and stepping back. The full transcript would be very lengthy and probably boring to read, since all the themes have been introduced, except one: a few people comment on the fact that Lisa (Lena's younger sister) was such a cute, curly-headed, adorable child. Lena wasn't and several speakers express a wondering, slightly guilty feeling that perhaps the trouble started right there. But the affirmation of caring, the feeling that there shouldn't be any blaming, the helplessness and the determination to be of help, and the theme that Lena has a real problem are all repeated. The room stays quiet. It is hard to believe, listening to the tape, that this is the same group that was so loud and vociferous earlier.

The intensity of concentration is real, as everyone listens to everyone else. And the feeling that it is important to take a turn and to say one's say is not just an effort to please the intervenors. It is something that everyone shares—almost as though the public "confession" clears the decks for the action to come. The sobbing and crying subside naturally, leaving everyone in a state of relaxed exhaustion—after having shared and experienced the depression they were warding off during the earlier resistance, and the attacks on the team and the technique.

This might be a good place to stop for a moment and comment on the different face that psychosis presents when it is seen in the network. For it manifests itself differently in a network than it does either in the family or in the one-to-one clinic visit. A psychiatrist sits down with a person labeled schizophrenic and after a few meetings, there will probably be very tight affects. The psychiatrist will be listening for delusional material. He will be very awkward and uncomfortable, which he'll notice in his countertransference. The patient will feel the same way. If you took a picture of them, both would look very strained. Take that same person and interview him with his family, and you may get some of those vibrations—but more often you will notice ordinary problems in communication. These are often very difficult to make really lucid and clear.

When you put the same family into a network, it is very hard to decide whose thought processes are out of whack. In the network, it's as though the person has been externalized into a social matrix that normalizes him—sheltering him and walling him off from himself and his family.

Lena, for instance, is hard for this group to understand as "crazy." She is the type of schizophrenic person whose symptoms are not especially bizarre: preoccupation with herself, withdrawal, somatic preoccupations, an active fantasy life, and hypochondriasis (a fear of heart attacks). The delusional system is not too well elaborated, although she gets paranoid at times—erupting with anger and aggression, threatening to kill people, and fearing that other people might kill her in turn. It's a not-uncommon pattern, similar to Janet's. The two girls did a lot of talking off to one side during the sessions, and it was helpful to both of them.

Some of the things that bothered the network were Lena's flatness of affect, her concreteness, and her lack of an elaborate symptom complex that they could grab hold of. There was a vagueness about her, which the professionals saw as a symptom. But it was hard for the network to distinguish this behavior from their own everyday experience. Some of them did begin to grasp that if she couldn't kiss her mother and cry like the rest of them, then maybe there was something in the communication pattern with her family that kept her from it. This wasn't a crystal clear insight, but it was the entering wedge in the breakthrough to come.

Having clarified these points, let's return to the transcript.

(It is still quiet; a few people have gotten a drink, or gone to the bathroom. The heavy crying is over, but no one wants

*to feel left out. Lena and Janet are back—on the floor with
the younger people, watching and thoughtful. For about an
hour people have been coming up to the parents and speaking, and we resume with the last few comments. The mix
of reactions has remained about the same throughout. Some
people have been very emotional—crying, embracing, and
barely able to talk. Some were wordy and almost pompous.
Nearly all were reassuring. By now it is the people on the
periphery of the room who are lined up—coming forward
and then making their way back to their places.*

OLDER WOMAN: *(Tearfully)* I remember how much the two
little girls puzzled you. Lena was always into things, and
Lisa was always so good. I don't mean goody-good, but
. . . well, Lena seemed to enjoy getting dirty and fighting,
and it made it hard to show her you loved her. . . . *(Sobs
heavily)* I don't know, of course, but it seems to me that
was the start of the problem . . . and none of us knew it
would be so hard. . . . *(Embraces Ruth and pats Ben)*

URI: Thank you. Next. . . .

YOUNGER WOMAN: I really haven't known either of you long
enough to know you either as people or as parents, but I
have known Lena for a while. . . . But I am young enough
to remember being a child, and I think that whenever a
problem exists, it's most important to sit down and calmly
talk it over. And from everything I've seen, you are both
intelligent people . . . and that when the emotion drains
away you'll be able to do that. . . .

URI: Next . . . next.

ANOTHER YOUNGER WOMAN: I feel a little strange because
I don't know you well, and I hate to butt in. . . . But it
seems to me that you've done too much for Lena, and she
hasn't had a chance to develop responsibility . . . but she
can! Maybe she ought to live away for a few months and
give yourselves a rest.

MATRONLY WOMAN: Ben you are so kind—and Ruth I feel for you because I feel she is sick . . . and it must be very hard. . . .

WOMAN: *(Another of the golfing parents)* I think you do need help . . . and maybe a separation from Lena, if we could figure out how to do it.

MAN: *(In his 40's)* I've been a witness to love . . . your love for Lena . . . and I hate to see you like this. I . . . I'd like to share the problem . . . really I do want to help. . . .

MAN: *(One of the professional types)* If this doesn't demonstrate love to your daughter . . . and to you . . . I don't know what does. . . . I think I realize that sometimes we bite our tongues a little more than we should . . . as parents and as friends . . . because if we don't, these young kids take every disagreement and turn it back into hostility. . . . And it's hard, but we have to keep doing it again and again and again. . . .

(He sighs deeply, places his hand on theirs for a minute, and turns away—fighting tears.)

YOUTH: *(In his 20's)* I really don't know what to say . . . except right now I love you . . . and I think Lisa's a nice girl . . . *(Catches himself)* and I think *Lena's* a nice girl! And strangely I think you've done a good job with your children . . . and whatever problems Lena's having right now, I don't think it's your fault. I don't think it's her fault either . . . I don't even think its a psychiatric fault. . . . Maybe it's a physiological fault, who knows . . . but certainly it's not your fault.

OLDER MAN: I don't think I know enough to tell you what's wrong with your family . . . I . . . think you're great people. . . .

MAN: *(In his 50's)* I don't suppose it helps, but I keep thinking that someday Lena will have a family of her own, and then maybe she'll know how you feel . . . But I don't think anyone who hasn't raised a family can understand what . . . what you're going through. . . .

WOMAN: *(In her 30's)* I just want you to know we are the kind of people you can call at 3 o'clock in the morning if you have to. . . .

WOMAN: *(High squeaky voice, probably from her own tension)* It just doesn't seem to me it's one person's fault . . . or another's. . . . And I just wish I knew how to help. . . .

MAN: I don't know exactly what to say . . . because . . . well, I just don't.

WOMAN: Ruth . . . Ben . . . *(Touches each as she speaks)* I am feeling very strange. . . . When you called and said you needed help, I didn't want to come . . . I didn't really understand what you meant by that . . . I guess I still don't . . . but I'm glad I'm able to tell you I'm here. . . .

URI: Two girls in the back there . . . you are the last ones, I think.

GIRL: *(About 30)* Ben, Ruth—you haven't made any mistake that I can think of. . . . I just don't know what to suggest. . . .

URI: Thank you—and how about you?

(A girl in her 20's comes up self-consciously and reaches out both hands to the couple.)

GIRL: Ruth, Ben . . . I know as a daughter, I've had conflicts with my parents . . . at times . . . and yet there was never a situation . . . a working out like this one. . . . I know that I'm glad my babies seem as normal as blueberry pie . . . but that doesn't mean that I think you've done wrong. . . . Why your daughter is sick, I really don't know . . . but don't blame yourself so much.

URI: There's maybe one or two more . . . what about you over there?

(The room stays hushed. No one is left who hasn't come up.)

URI: Well thank you very much. I'm going to ask you to do something very different now . . . involving those people Lena started choosing a while ago—and Lena. Will you all come up here please? . . .

(Ruth and Ben look up, blinking from having kept their heads down for the long and mostly eyes-closed vigil; they move back the sofa. Uri and the rest of the team are clearing the central space of chairs. As he gives directions, most of the group sits shaking themselves—as if coming out of a long dream. They remain quiet and attentive. He takes Lena by the hand and goes about helping her select—or accept—a group of about 12 or 15 people. They are all aged 45 or younger—including Larry, Joshua, Susan, and Sara, as well as a number of others identified by the team as vigorous, potential activists. As soon as they are gathered together—and before much talking in the wider audience can begin—Uri claps his hands and gets attention. He and Lena join hands, and the group forms a circle.)

URI: The task is for this group, first of all, to just sway for a while.

(He and Lena begin, and after a few ripples, the group begins to sway together in a slow rhythm. This lasts only a minute or two before further directions are given. The group looks relaxed and unified.)

URI: I think that's about enough now—we feel united. . . . The task is rather simple . . . at least I hope it is. . . . Maybe it's more complicated, but I hope it is easy enough for all of you.

(He shifts his position so that Lena is forced to step into the circle. He steps back and maneuvers so that, as he breaks the circle, the persons next to him put their arms around each other's shoulders. The others shift to locked arms or shoulders almost automatically.)

URI: Lena, you have all these people in a ring around you,

and . . . and your task, whether you like it or not, is to break through the circle and get out. . . . You can use any means you like . . . as long as you don't kill anyone. . . . Your task is to get out—and the task of the group is not to let you out. . . . If she gets out, fine . . . but don't let her. . . .

LENA: Uh . . . are they ready?

URI: Come on now, let's start. . . . Get yourself out of there.

VOICES: *(Murmuring)* Come on now. . . . Be careful. . . . Watch it. . . .

(Lena dashes one way and another—testing a bit—then tries to part the interlocked arms. She darts about for a few minutes, then stops—puzzled, and panting.)

LARRY: Come on Lena, get up.

(She tries butting, shoving, and even a tentative bite. Her face gets red, and she begins to sweat—then stops to pant a moment. Uri immediately urges her on.)

URI: Come on now—get out! Let's go.

(She begins to kick and pound with her fists—darting frantically, trying for a weak place. The circle staggers together and moves around the space a bit, sometimes bumping chairs or tables, but not letting go. Ross and a couple of other team members are watching closely—propping up the perimeter at its weak points, or clearing the path. The circle members are grunting and panting; people on the outside are cheering Lena on—with Uri's encouragement.)

URI: Come on! . . . Get out! . . . Break out! . . .

(The group and Lena stop for breath periodically, but Uri never allows this for more than 20 or 30 seconds. After about ten minutes, Lena decides that one of the women represents a weak link. She lowers her head and charges, while the woman doubles over to protect her abdomen from a hard, butting collision. Lena almost makes it over the top—and at that moment, Ross grabs her shoulders, and Uri grabs

her feet. They lift her over the heads of the circle and set her down on the floor outside. There is an outbreak of excitement. The larger group comments excitedly, while those in the circle drop their grip on one another, smile, laugh, rub their bruises, and catch their breath. Lena is dazed and surprised.)

ROSS: *(Shouts)* Hey, you're out . . . you're out!

(He fosters applause and cheering from all sides.)

URI: *(After about a minute)* Now let's get the circle together again. There's one more task before us. Now that you are out, you must break in. . . . Let's go. . . .

(The circle re-forms—again facing inward.)

LENA: How?

URI: Any way you can think of . . . Come on now, get going.

(Lena tries first to pull the circle apart; then she gets down and tries to go between legs. She fights—pounding and pulling and pushing all around the circle. There are screams of "ow" and "oooh" from women in the group. Once Lena backs off—nearly knocking down one of the bystanders—and says, "Oh, excuse me. . . .")

URI: *(Cuts in)* Don't worry about it. . . . Let's go.

(The circle remains in a tight huddle. After about five minutes, Lena starts trying to climb over the top. Uri and Ross again aid her to success—shoving her from behind so that she falls unceremoniously on the floor in the center. For a long moment, she sits staring up at the circle of grinning faces—who stare back at her in amazement. Then they drop arms and burst into a long shared laugh, with Lena joining in. As the applause breaks out, Uri jumps in and cuts it off.)

URI: Lena. Close your eyes . . . stay where you are, and shut your eyes. . . . Now each of you go up to her, and touch her, and tell her what you are feeling. Right now. Go ahead.

(The members of the circle go up to her eagerly—expressing a physical and emotional closeness from having shared the experience.)

LARRY: I didn't think you could, but you did it. Good for you!

MAN: You're a good girl.

ELSIE: Boy are you gutsy!

SUSAN: Atta girl!

JOSHUA: Boy, what a ball player you'd make.

WOMAN: First time you've come out and worked for something in a long time . . . and you have real guts.

MAN: Boy, what a fighter.

WOMAN: *(Out of breath—hugging her)* Whew . . . how about that!

URI: *(Rounds up the spectators)* Come on now—everybody . . . just as you did with Ben and Ruth.

(Most of the comments are lost as the group mills around, but the general tone is friendly and admiring—with much hugging and embracing. One of the circle members brings Lena a cold drink, as numerous small-group conversations spring up. The talk builds in pitch, until it is as loud as the pre-meeting hubbub. But this is different. Whereas before, the chitchat was social and tended to defuse anxieties, or mask them, people have now shared several deeply moving and involving experiences. They talk to one another without their social masks—just relating—and begin to speculate and plan. There is less formality about going up to Lena, and sometimes several people come up at once. After a while, she moves over to a chair, where people still seek her out and tell her how they admired her efforts—and how strong, brave, and determined she seems to be.

As the group seems well into this phase, Ross unplugs his tape recorder, Uri gets his coat on, and the team wanders out—almost unnoticed by anyone in the room. It's a little

*after 11 o'clock, and its been a long session. But the change
in the atmosphere is palpable. The network is now open to
all kinds of possibilities, and the depression and anger with
which the evening began has dissipated considerably. It is
time to allow the network to function on its own for another
week.)*

Postsession Developments and Comments

It is hard to know whether the preceding pages convey to the
reader the ebb and flow of activity, the intensity, and the
emotional quality of the network session. If there is a certain
sense of disjointedness, a sense of some things getting started,
but not chased down and pushed into form, then one of the
essentials of the technique has been transmitted. This aspect
of the intervention process has been stressed before. It
emerged most strongly at the beginning, in the dialectic
efforts to polarize the group and make clear to the assembled
family, friends, and neighbors that it was up to them, and not
the leaders, to develop strategies and accomplish the task of
helping this family.

However, the real concern and sense of responsibility on
the part of Uri, Ross, and the team should also be apparent.
The use of the two encounter techniques was carefully
planned; and there would be some question about using them
in some other groups. For instance, the breaking in and out
of the circle is a much more intense emotional experience
when one is surrounded by friends and family, rather than
a group of strangers. It is also physically strenuous. The
members of the circle were carefully chosen and inducted
into participation by the team because of their potential as
activists in the resolution of Lena's problems and those of her
parents. But the team also took care that no one chosen

appeared to be heart-attack prone or unable to take the stress involved. A certain amount of security was provided by the presence of at least five M.D.'s, besides the psychiatrist. Despite their challenge to the psychiatrist and his methods, the physicians had been willing to consult with him professionally about the state of health of the members. The father's physician, particularly, was able to give an opinion that Ben could stand emotional strain of a fairly intense nature for a single evening—which permitted the team to apply their strategies.

Those who have tried to relate this session to the previous theoretical descriptions will recognize the phases of polarization and mobilization, and also the thorough way in which the depression had to be dealt with before the group could move on. The quickness and impact of the group during the breakthrough activities with Lena is typical of this phase, when it occurs within a session.

Some readers will look for retribalization techniques at the beginning of the session. In point of fact, this session occurred before the theoretical formulation was developed, and before there was explicit awareness of the value of ritualizing this element. A suggestion of its potency is found in the brief moment of swaying together by the circle and Lena, before she attempted to break out. Whether or not a retribalization ritual could have been developed for this particular network is a matter for speculation. A review of the transcript suggests that verbal sparring between the resistant professional network members and the team might have served as such a ritual for this network. There is still much research to be done in this area, but the record of this early session affords us the satisfaction of finding most of the theoretical phases of the cycle evident. Analysis of other tapes and of new applications of the principles and methods is a task that should be joined by many in the future.

After this session, the activist group began to apply much more pressure to get Lena out of her isolation. One of the girls in the network had her own apartment, although she was only 19. She invited Lena to live with her for a while. This was pretty difficult since Lena still didn't have a job, or anything to do, but it was a beginning. When Lena returned home, Joshua and Susan had a job for her, and the network members saw to it that she went to work regularly for about three months. That fall, the Dallas branch of the family arranged for her to enter a college near them, and she was finally able to make a geographic break with her family. Her course through school was erratic, but she finished, and she is now working regularly (and dating) for the first time in her life. She is also able to visit home from time to time without being driven back into her symptomatic behavior.

The parents, too, received much attention. As the masks were dropped, it became obvious that everyone in the family had the capacity for violence and quarrelsomeness that Lena openly flaunted. Family fights were vigorous, with ashtrays being thrown, furniture broken, and considerable vituperation exposed. The activists moved in to cool out these battles and bring some of the points at issue to resolution.

The network continued to meet for over a year—not always in such great numbers, or on a weekly basis. The bonds of friendship and relationship remain strong, and many of the binds between network members have been relaxed through this participation. Perhaps sparked by the local newspaper column, Lena began publishing a network newsletter the week following the session. It seems fitting to close this report with a quotation from an issue some months later: "The summer vacation has eaten into the attendance, but Lena is working now and needs us a little less. . . ."

APPENDIX

Consulting and Teaching
Techniques of Social
Network Assembly

IN ORDER to learn how networks function, and particularly the techniques and concepts appropriate to large network assembly, the aspiring intervenor must have some direct experience. Initially, we relied on didactic sessions interwoven with team apprenticeship during the course of selecting and carrying through several assembly interventions. But the advantages of apprenticeship and participatory learning seemed muffled by several other aspects of reality. For one thing, overly large teams diluted the experience to an observational one for trainees. Those whose learning style was especially vigorous did assume responsibility and managed to participate in the interventions. But most apprentices were understandably diffident and reluctant to assert themselves during the sessions. Conflicting theoretical models of the goals of psychotherapy and differing perceptions of individual and dyadic interactions presented further problems. And when training experience is interwoven on a schedule that interrupts other clinic activities frequently—but is still too brief for the team of aspirants to experience the network

140

effect acting upon themselves—then the training becomes uphill work.

At this point, we feel that there are as many challenges to teaching as there are to intervening, and that a variety of approaches is needed so that each group may have opportunities that fit their needs as well as their expectations. Whatever the training modality, a combination of at least a few of the following kinds of prior experience will be helpful: personal analysis or therapy; treatment of psychotics; family therapy; long-term group therapy, with an emphasis on pathology; and brief, intense psychotherapy along the lines of encounter groups, with an emphasis on the complex capacities of the normal human being. An eclectic position enhances one's ability to utilize selectively multiple skills as the need arises.

Over the last several years, we have had experience with lectures and verbal discussions that try to teach how to assemble social networks for intervention. Many people are interested and intrigued. They begin to become aware of their own social networks and those surrounding the persons in their clinical practice. They are able to get an intellectual understanding of the important role that social processes and social pathology play in the troubles in people's lives. However, the lecture-seminar-anecdotal method does not necessarily lead to the communication of the network effect. The experience of large tribal assemblies must become a personal referent before one shifts comfortably from cognitive to active employment of this style of intervention. This is necessary because the retribalization phenomenon needs to be distinguished from other group experiences. Even though it may make use of related skills and recognize similar landmarks, the phenomenon is different in essence and application from other therapeutic modalities.

While social network concepts can be applied to many

clinical situations, we have noted earlier that the large tribal assembly, with all of its dramatic implications, is only feasible in severe crisis, when simpler methods of therapy and intervention have failed or seem to be inadequate. And while apprenticeship may be the ideal learning experience, real-life crises cannot be scheduled on alternate Thursdays at 10:00 A.M. to meet the training needs of aspiring professionals. Nevertheless, neophyte network intervenors should have a live experience with network assemblies before crises erupt in their caseload.

Since professional scheduling for a team of four or five members is complex, and crisis situations are by definition unpredictable, we have found that the network effect can be readily simulated to give a group of professionals an opportunity for learning. This requires a conference or seminar of 40 to 50 professional people, for a minimum of three hours of uninterrupted activity. The theory and practice of this technique of teaching network assembly and intervention is built upon and utilizes the same ingredients that master teachers have used down through the centuries. It is closely related to the training for other modalities of therapy such as psychodrama, family therapy, and group and individual counseling. Its greater effectiveness in contrast to pure lecture discussion methods can be perceived in the following example.

A Network Simulation Experience

A group of family therapists in a large eastern city got in touch with us because they wanted to observe a social network intervention. They suggested that we bring a tribal assembly to them so that they could get the feel of the process. When the logistical impossibilities of doing this were clarified, the group then agreed to our suggestion that, since they were already a type of network, our team could simulate a network assembly and intervention using their own staff. We could in this way provide them with the experience of feeling the process, the techniques, and the network effect— if they would provide a three-hour session, and if they would guarantee an attendance of at least 45 staff members and colleagues.

As this particular group was composed primarily of people whose greatest training was in family therapy, the intervention process was enhanced, since it was unnecessary to fill in cognitively their awareness of the influence of extended family members upon individuals. Simulation was also facilitated because the group was familiar with role relationships and role-playing techniques. However, only a few of the group had participated in any extensive lecture discussion or reading about social network assembly and intervention. Just as every network is unique, every training situation is unique and requires minor variations in actual simulation. In this instance, we decided to set the stage by first giving a half-hour lecture on the theory of network assembly, intervention, and the six phases that occur in natural sequence.

Since the meeting places for simulation are usually formal lecture halls or similar rooms, rather than homes, it is important to utilize space and seating in a way that approximates the actual experience. With this family therapy group, we elected to remove half or more of the chairs so as to allow half of the group to sit on the floor. The others were forced to move their chairs out of stiff rows in order to have closer eye contact with the leader, who was on the floor, too. Our simulation begins by reorganizing time, space, and social distance away from the ritualized professional roles. This elicits an early appearance of network relationships, as the learning group copes with these new situations—emitting a variety of interesting protests and reactions.

Following the lecture, the group was instructed to form simulated families of at least four to six persons, each of which would develop a family problem of sufficient severity to indicate network intervention. They were to work out role relationships that could be sustained for the afternoon. We have found that about half an hour of role and problem rehearsal is ample time for this process to become established. Longer family simulations tend to become static or stilted. While the families are gathering themselves together, team teaching intervenors mingle on the periphery, facilitating the role development and selecting one family that seems suitable to use as the index unit for the network assembly to follow.

One needs to expect resistance in any setting, but especially among professionals, who exhibit a particularly stubborn reluctance to engage in simulated experience. First, simulation confronts sophisticated professional inhibitions. Second, a majority of professionals find the reversal of roles —from therapist to patient—uncomfortable, especially in the presence of their peers. The facilitation of the network effect begins as these resistances are met and the participants are inducted into their roles. Once they are well into the roles, the freedom to indulge in behaviors allowed only to their patients is intoxicating. Most professionals find the improvisational experience exciting and satisfying.

In this instance, an appropriate family group volunteered to be the index family, and the others were announced as their kin and neighbors. We were now ready to initiate the network assembly intervention. We have noted that retribalization is the first phase in every creation of a viable social network—and simulated interventions are no exception. The network was called to order, as it would have been in a home, and the conductor gave a short talk modeled after the remarks that would have been made to a real collection of family, kin, neighbors, and friends. Then the group was asked to stand, and its members were encouraged to yell and shout until full participation of the network was achieved. At this point, they further relaxed by holding hands and swaying with their eyes closed.

The next step was a move towards polarization. The index family was asked to sit in the center of the room and present their problem, and the rest of the network was instructed to listen and await the chance to react aloud. Almost always, the index family effectively arouses polarization in this maneuver because of the rigid role structure that occurs in pathological families. Simulated problem families are no exception, and those familiar with family therapy often accelerate the process in their role projection.

The rest of the network, which is forced to observe but not participate, experiences a buildup of frustrations with the family, which bursts forth when released by the teaching leader. They usually begin to comment in an impatient and imperious tone, which has now lost any vestige of acting or simulation.

In this instance, the index family was reacting inappropriately to their 19-year-old pregnant and unmarried daughter. When the network had its turn to respond to the family problems, several network members mimed the family by making sarcastic and flippant suggestions. Then one social worker in the outer network, who worked in an adoption agency, started to admonish the family for their handling of the daughter. She then went into a very personal diatribe against the whole assembled group, saying: "You people are professionals, and you are disgusting me. Don't you realize that there are so many unloved children in the world? The

younger generation today is totally irresponsible with the
pill, abortions, and neglecting their infants! Now you people
are saying it's all right if we have hundreds of thousands of
un-cared-for babies. Shame on you!"

This illustrates how a professional role in an agency or
clinic can fuse with a role in a network simulation; the experience can become very personal, as the training experience
breaks through conscious control and loses its artificiality.
This role fusion aids in transmitting a sense of the timing of
the phases of social network intervention. Polarization, for
instance, can be brought about in many ways. In general, the
network intervenor relies on the natural antipathies and at-
tractions that occur in all large groups and catalyzes and
selectively focuses the polarization around topics that are
germane to the network and to the simulated family. Polarization intensifies group feelings and makes the network
members impatient and ready to get something done. It thus
sets the stage for the mobilization of the activists.

In this network training assemblage, the intervenor and
the network began focusing on three problems that the index
family had exposed: the "illegitimate" pregnancy, the drug
problems of the teenage siblings, and the neighborhood drug
culture—which seemed especially intrusive because the
family were relative newcomers to the state. The network
became excited when one of the members suggested that
what the family and the neighborhood needed was a super-
vised coffee house, where teenagers could get together under
some adult supervision. An outline was sketched suggesting
a plan bridging the generation gap between the older and
younger members of the neighborhood. As the activists began mobilizing, a few verbal fights occurred between
"friends" and "relatives" in the peripheral network, during
which family secrets were exposed just as in real-life networks.

The depression phase was marked by the index family's stubborn resistance to suggestions and offers of help from various members and clusters of the larger group; the family had chosen a particularly frustrating defensive role structure, which rendered the entire assembly either impotent or simply ineffectual at times.

After about an hour and a half of interactive dialogue between family and network members, a positive group feeling emerged that seemed to result from decreased resistance by the index family to suggestions for altering their own role images. In addition, some feeling of accomplishment relaxed the peripheral network. They now sensed that by effort and sheer force of numbers, they had made themselves heard and could be of help. This is the breakthrough phase, which in an actual network assembly, is followed by activity whose momentum persists between sessions. During a simulated assembly, it is marked by an "aha" of insight, as the sense of the experience integrates with self and former learnings. This produces an excitement that leads quickly to elation-exhaustion and a sense of new mastery. In effect, the simulation has become a mechanism through which all the network members have begun to participate in further learning.

With this particular group, there had been some abstract, highly intellectualized questions after the initial brief lecture. In contrast, after the network simulation experience, excitement ran high. The discussion that followed for the next half hour ran past the formal dismissal time. Interactions among the group had the qualities of depth, insight, and lively personal understanding. These qualities are noticeably absent after purely intellectual and cognitive presentations of the technique.

The reader will recall the earlier expectations of those few members of the group who had read and thought about network assembly as a form of therapeutic intervention.

They had remained sufficiently naïve, in spite of their understanding, to request that a network be brought to them. Now this same group suggested that they might form their own team of network intervenors and begin to try learning together with selected cases. Since they had integrated their reading with the direct learning experience of the simulation, they saw no reason why they could not do their own tribal assembly when the next appropriate clinical crisis presented itself.

Not all simulation training experiences can be completed in a single half-day. In the case of a much less experienced staff, three sessions were used because the cognitive and technical framework had to be established before the simulation itself could have sufficient impact. Each request for training, teaching, and demonstration needs to be evaluated as carefully as does a request for therapeutic intervention. Our experience suggests that simulation is the key training modality, and that it can be integrated with apprenticeship and other teaching modes.

Once this direct learning has occurred, and cognitive understanding integrates with insight, additional learning and practice can be developed efficiently. It might be possible to organize teams of varying degrees of experience in many cities, with consultation and supervision shared widely by senior interventionists. Although we speculated earlier about the viability of a single team giving full time to this type of practice, another possibility emerges. A veteran of several assembled and simulated network experiences may find it possible to consult or act as leader to a team gathered locally on an episodic basis. Something along these lines seems to be a viable option and is very much in tune with the crisis nature of network assembly situations. Just as former activists under team direction can implode new networks, of which they are not natural members, so less experienced professionals can in this way gain apprenticeship training while giving meaningful service. The team of intervenors can become nuclear members of a professional network that can replicate itself, rather than transport itself intact.

As there are more and more people gaining experience with network intervention, there will be many occasions and requests to share expertise in a training capacity. Any would-be teacher in the field needs to watch out for the pitfall of the hidden agenda. Often part of a staff or institution wants to work on its own pathology in the guise of learning to help others. This leads to much resistance to participation in simulated roles, and could render the training session sterile as a learning exercise.

In some instances, it may be wise to leave the artificiality of the simulation apparent in order to allow for cognitive learning without pushing the staff too fast or too hard. The teaching intervenor has to feel in control of the process so that he or she can accelerate or slow down the interactions appropriately. These decisions can only be made by a clinician who has had substantial experience with the technique. Just as assembling a network is not for amateurs, neither should the teaching of this intervention modality be approached glibly. While it is exciting and attractive to engage the currents of real-life problems, the experienced social network intervenor knows that it is not worthwhile to stir people up simply for the sake of muddying the waters.

Network Interventions in Professional Associations and Other Institutions

From previous experience, we have learned that institutional hierarchies have many similarities to extended family social network hierarchies. So it would seem that if institutional power structures are amenable to and hopeful for change, a combination of techniques in the context of social network intervention might offer something to improve the state of institutional health.

We have been consulted a number of times by officers of professional associations who were concerned about the viability and future of their organizations. These professionals had conceptualized themselves as a peer network, and we were given the opportunity to attempt a network assembly intervention when the members met together at some normal function. The hidden agenda was the goal of revitalizing the association. It is interesting that the officers of these groups were acutely aware of the problems and distress of their members, but were usually blind to the defects in the organizational structure and its processes for which they were responsible. Officers and senior members tend to blame themselves at the same time that they complain about the lack of involvement of the general membership—just as parents flounder in efforts to understand and engage their offspring.

As in contemporary society itself, two frequent problems in professional organizations are the reluctance of elder statesmen to relinquish control, and the lack of awareness by the available maturing younger generation of options short of symbolic murder. This can be seen in any group when offices and responsibilities are passed around a small circle. Rigidities of this type, which result in an impasse every time change is attempted, are symptoms. In essence, they indicate defective relationships between process and structure rather than a lack of interest on the part of the younger people, or power mania on the part of the elders. The exhausted senior member often wants help as badly as newer members want to give it.

One reason for this breakdown lies in the tendency of older

people to pay more attention to linkages with higher authority than do younger people. As a result, they tend to perpetuate an increasing complexity of rules, regulations, and rituals, which then become the rationalizations and excuses for being unable to change the organization. One such organization of about 40 members—a local unit with a national affiliation—had been complaining among themselves that their group was dying on the vine. In a network consultation, it was disclosed that only five people were technically eligible for top office. Previously, they had been blaming their institutional lethargy on the unwillingness of the rank and file to take responsibility. But suddenly the polarization shifted to a conflict between local operating needs and formal national rules. The absurdity of the situation became apparent when younger members pointed out that duly elected officers of the local society had been prevented from taking office because the national organization had refused to accept their credentials. Unlike the local group, the national superstructure had not changed with the times and was imposing quite different requirements for membership.

When the problem was seen realistically by the assembly, mobilization was possible around new options. Both the older and younger members of the organization could accept the usefulness of establishing themselves as separate from the national association. Another possible tactic was to gather strength for forcing a change at the national level, which would benefit all the local branches. The energizing effect of these insights enabled new relationships to become viable.

A useful technique for giving the entire professional group a sense of its own interdependence and transgenerational qualities is to end this type of network assembly on a note of solidarity. This can be accomplished by a steamlined "sculpting" of the history of the group. A large area of a room is cleared of furniture, the oldest founding member is asked to bring forward the first persons he initiated into the "tribe." Each of these in turn bring forward those that they inducted, and this is continued until the newest "children" from the periphery have joined the chain. Seen from outside, the effect is that of a tribal portrait. An actual photograph taken at this point will help complete the retribalization and is more meaningful to the participants than many of the ceremonially posed group photographs that accumulate as souvenirs and quasi-historical documents.

It is surprising how much easier it is for elder statesmen to release their tight grip on the reins and allow the younger members to become workhorses—even to support new innovations with enthusiasm—once they have experienced this group acknowledgment of their particular place in its history. The older generation no longer feels cut adrift on an ice floe, and the young turks are no longer burdened with the necessity of "killing" their fathers. The tribe has a history, and change becomes part of growth instead of having to be denied.

Whenever we have been involved in efforts to reduce alienation, free creative energy, and evolve viable social structures, the same sequence of mood and activity phases occurs. Healing seems to take place in both individuals and groups through the learning climate that we have tried to describe as both a therapeutic intervention and a teaching method.

The Problem of Fees and Payment

Social network intervention is too new to be recognized by most fee-setting schedules—whether in agencies, governmental reimbursement schedules, or insurance company definitions. Yet, without such third-party payments, social network fees—like fees for analysis—could be prohibitive for any but the rich. Since upper-income families and networks do not have a greater need for network intervention than either poor families or families of average income, the fee is a very serious problem. The discussion that follows is only the very unsatisfactory beginnings of a solution.

Until this therapeutic method becomes well established, each network intervention team will have to work out its own methods for arriving at practical billing estimates and collection procedures. Some insurance companies will pay for contact hours of professional time, and can be billed according to the discipline of each team member. But many companies will balk at multiple fees charged to one patient's bill. As a matter of fact, their logic is correct. For one of the principles of social network intervention is that if there is any "patient," it is the total network—not a single individual. It is warping to one's conscience, and sometimes emotionally nauseating, to write bills and complete forms that (with a classical diagnostic code) spotlight one individual who dramatizes the network's distress—labeling him "sick."

Some teams have entertained the idea of asking network members, or at least the extended family, to share the costs. While this has some rational basis, it is doubtful if a network intervention team would find it very comfortable to carry this suggestion to its logical conclusion and charge an admission fee for each session (let alone be able to collect it).

However, some inventive solution will have to be found unless the whole system of fees and payments can be changed. By usual standards, professional contact time for a team of three would total at least $50 per hour—and considerably more in many cases. If a series of six network sessions and consultation time between sessions totaled 30 hours, the bill would be $1500. Compared to the cost of 18 months of psychotherapy, or three to five years of psychoanalysis, or lifelong institutionalization, the final bill does not seem excessive. However, families, agencies, and insurance companies seldom make this comparison. In fact, in view of the relatively short time span involved, and the assignment of responsibility for change to network members themselves, it often seems to outsiders as though this sum is exorbitant. Until realistic cost analysis can be used, without the constraints of the medical model—which uses one individual as the basic unit—no realistic solution to the economic problem can be offered. Each intervention team will have to struggle with the problem of how to set fees that are fair to both the networks and the team members. Sometimes it will be better to compromise than to insist on being adequately compensated.

Records and Confidentiality.

Naturally some records have to be kept during the course of an intervention, since the complexity of events and the speed of their development often tax human memory. Later, this raw data is also useful for theory building, but its collection and storage raise a few ethical problems.

Within the network itself, with almost no exceptions, there should be no secrets. In fact, part of the effectiveness of social network intervention involves opening up communication channels within the network so that members experience some relief from their private burdens and develop trust in one another. The fear of exposing secrets that some subsystems of the network may have been holding onto tenaciously and often self-destructively—in spite of their good intentions

—is often one of the major barriers to giving and receiving help. A good deal of energy is bound up in preserving these distorted half-truths, as any psychotherapist knows. When secrets are disclosed in the presence of the network, the attendant relief frees the group to do its work. This not only generates excitement, it provides the opportunity for the total system to develop new options on a realistic basis. This process may be one of the crucial sources of energy in the drive past the depressive resistant phase to breakthrough— enabling the activists to be effective.

Social network assemblies involving from 40 to 200 persons at one time, usually in crisis situations where other simpler methods have failed, start with the thesis that the crisis cannot be solved unless there is no confidentiality, no secrecy, and no privacy. As we have indicated, this is explicitly stated both to the nuclear persons who are the primary target of the network effect and to the assembled social network. However, it must be realized that tensions are running high, and an emotional aura surrounds the tribe, so many persons in the network will not really hear this statement. There is a tendency to regard the network process as merely an extension of ordinary one-to-one therapy that the network member has been invited to witness. A denial defense is also operating, so that at first no one realizes that any particular network person may open himself up and reveal intimate and personal things in such a large assembly. From observation, it does not appear to us that any "informed consent" could be secured, even if it were attempted. Perhaps in their public nature, network meetings share this problem with Pentecostal churches, A.A. groups, some drug rehabilitation communities, and other tribalizing assemblies.

However, those engaged in social network intervention should anticipate that inevitably they are going to be confronted at some time by individuals who may be disturbed about their own or someone else's exposure and revelations in the assembly. Although few states recognize professional confidentiality for psychiatrists, confidentiality for priests and lawyers is almost universal. But the public image of psychiatry is such that the average person believes he has inviolate rights to privacy, secrecy, and confidentiality with his psychiatrist. We believe that this should be so in the one-to-one situation. We also believe it is impossible in any group situation, including the marital dyad, the family, and to a greater extent, the assembly of a social network.

Whenever this issue of confidentiality has been raised, our position has been to point out that an assembled network is not an individual, that everyone gossips—even after A. A. meetings and the like—and that any social network, when traced to its furthest limits, travels around the world. If an individual persists in being anxious, his only recourse is to drop out of the network. A few paranoid persons may do so, but most remain and profit from the experience.

As we have shown, there is a sound theoretical basis for insisting upon openness, directness, and lack of confidentiality when dealing with social networks. The pathological social network owes most of its rigidity and inflexibility to the presence of secrets, collusions, and alliances, which must be broken up in order for change to occur.

For this vital theoretical and practical set of reasons, we do not commonly request the signing of releases to permit recording, and the like. As a matter of fact, even in cases involving paranoid persons with recording phobias and suspicions focused on broadcasting, the contract of trust between the distressed persons and the team, reflected back into trust in the social network, is the circuit of choice.

When one is confident of this position, it is surprisingly simple for one of the team members to install a tape recorder in the room during the preassembly phase of the network session. Questions about it are handled in the same way that team identities are handled—simply, factually, but without lengthy explanation or apology. The use of thin tape and a recording speed of the slowest order, usually one and seven-eighths inches per second, is sufficient to record a four- or five-hour session on a single reel, without further attention. The complexity of the interactions among 40 or more people and the sheer quantity of events that transpire make any other recording system inadequate. The audio tape catches enough so that it can be analyzed and understood by those who were present. These recordings are often invaluable in debriefings and strategy sessions.

Legal and Ethical Problems of Publication

Although we do not follow tradition about confidentiality within the network session itself, some other professional traditions are crucial and must be observed. The right of the network to privacy from exposure to outsiders should be guarded in the same fashion that privacy in individual therapy has previously been safeguarded. The same ethical constraints apply to masking identities and keeping discussions professional, rather than temptingly titillating, whenever network cases are made public, whether in lecture, workshop, or print.

Records of network sessions must be subject to the same security precautions as any other clinical data. Without these precautions, the sense of trust in the team would evaporate, and the professional community would be appropriately concerned about the professional integrity of the team as colleagues.

Innovators in any field will be mercilessly approached by journals, reporters, free-lance writers, and others whose business is to bring to the attention of the public and practicing professionals the growing fringes of experimentation and knowledge. The vicars of the profession, sensing carelessness or afraid of scandal, can be expected to criticize the reporting of actual cases. They do have one point that needs to be heard: in certain ways, couples are more identifiable in print than are individuals; families are more identifiable than couples; and social networks are more identifiable than any of the preceeding. This is mainly because of the number of people involved.

Obviously, clinical techniques, procedures, and case examples will have to be published. The best protection for the persons involved is to change the locale and as many personal, identifying features as possible. Nevertheless, the network intervenor can expect to be chastised by certain persons who were present at any reported network intervention and who believe that since they can identify themselves and others, insufficient precautions were taken.

When a person goes into individual therapy, he may mention it to half a dozen friends and say a little bit about the therapist. This is limited information, and second-hand, it excites few people. However, if 50 persons participating in a network intervention each tell six friends, then 300 persons know something of what happened from a first-hand source. If each of them tells six more friends, then 1800 persons know a little about the network. The communication chain may stop at about this level, but people are always telephoning and writing letters, and news from afar often gets amplified. In a typical network, the news of some of the happenings reverberates back and forth from New York to California and across the ocean several times. As far as we are concerned, this is human nature, a network phenomenon, and has nothing whatsoever to do with legal issues.

What the network intervenor needs to know is that from time to time this kind of objection may be raised, and that he must be able to counteract it with wisdom and assurance. In such a situation, as in the session itself, there probably is no such thing as "informed consent." The effort to obtain signed permissions to publish material might give some measure of comfort to the professional, but it would be of little protection to the network. Attempts at formal releases seem to us potentially to raise such impossible issues that not only would publication in professional literature not occur, but the retribalization process would be seriously hampered if the network got bogged down in them.

Probably, it will not be long before there are network movies as well as television and videotape reports of tribal assemblies. Already, requests from filmmakers are persistent and numerous. The network intervenor will have to decide, both with the network and the production personnel, what legal safeguards have to be taken prior to the production or exhibition of such a film or video recording.

The closest parallels to the filming of network assemblies known to us are certain films that have been shot on location, in which most, if not all, of the actors were local people enlisted on the spot. At the premiere of one such film, Faulkner's *Intruder in the Dust,* one of us sat in the midst of townsfolk who played themselves. It was remarkable how well they accepted the harsh roles, and how few angry or reproachful comments were heard afterwards. It seemed that honest, recognizable interactions, even under stress, were acceptable. While it is a work of fiction, this film is an excellent example of real-life network processes presented by a keen observer, and is well worth study both for this content and for the bearing it has on future media treatment of network assemblies.

To return to practical filming problems, for purely professional presentation, signed permission by the nuclear family or local group in advance of production, and an explanation to the assembled network, may be sufficient. For public presentation, signed permission by all the network members will probably have to be obtained by the commercial source after the finished production is available.

Index

161